SPONGEBOB SQUAREPANTS

SPONGEBOB SQUAREPANTS

The Unauthorized FUN-ography

PAUL VOLPONI

ROWMAN & LITTLEFIELD
Lanham • Boulder • New York • London

Published by Rowman & Littlefield
An imprint of The Rowman & Littlefield Publishing Group, Inc.
4501 Forbes Boulevard, Suite 200, Lanham, Maryland 20706
www.rowman.com

86-90 Paul Street, London EC2A 4NE, United Kingdom

British Library Cataloguing in Publication Information Available

Library of Congress Cataloging-in-Publication Data Available

ISBN 978-1-5381-8029-7 (cloth : alk. paper) | ISBN 978-1-5381-8030-3 (ebook)

∞™ The paper used in this publication meets the minimum requirements of American National Standard for Information Sciences—Permanence of Paper for Printed Library Materials, ANSI/NISO Z39.48-1992.

CONTENTS

CONTENTS

INTRODUCTION

Stand on any street corner and randomly stop people walking past. Ask them, "Who lives at 1600 Pennsylvania Avenue?" Perhaps a third of them will respond, "That's the address of the White House in Washington, DC. The president of the United States lives there." The other two-thirds will most likely have no clue. Then ask those same people, "Who lives in a pineapple under the sea?" The overwhelming majority will smile widely and confidently reply—usually in a singsong, staccato style parodying the theme song—"SpongeBob SquarePants!"

That's the type of indelible impression SpongeBob has made on our society. The incredibly naive and purehearted fry cook who slings krabby patties at the Krusty Krab—Bikini Bottom's number-one fast-food restaurant—actually has made being a dork cool. Why have so many people gravitated to this silly, goody-goody character and invited SpongeBob and his surrounding cast of undersea characters into their living rooms and lives? The answer is quite simple: all that SpongeBob ever wanted from us was to be our friend. And that was enough to open the doors to our hearts.

Remarkably, the series *SpongeBob SquarePants* turns twenty-five years old in July 2024. In celebration of that event, this book traces the character's journey from the edges of a quiet tidal pool observed by creator, artist, and marine biologist Stephen Hillenburg to SpongeBob's current status as a media superstar. Is this a biography? Not really. Think of it more as a *fun-ography*. Why? Because unfettered fun has been the driving force behind every *SpongeBob* episode and film. So pull up your bright yellow socks. (You know, the ones subtly adorned with SpongeBob's face.) Get out your plush stuffies of the various characters, gather them closely around you, and settle in. Then prepare for a rollicking ride through Bikini Bottom. Don't worry, I've got the wheel—SpongeBob is still trying to get his boating license.

Better hurry now. I can hear SpongeBob in the front passenger seat chanting, "I'm ready! I'm ready! I'm ready!"

1

HAPPY, YELLOW, AND SQUARE (EVENTUALLY)

HUMBLE ORIGINS

Like most cartoon characters, SpongeBob went through several incarnations before he was introduced to the world at large. He was the brainchild of artist and marine biologist Stephen Hillenburg, who was born at Fort Sill, an army base in the landlocked state of Oklahoma, where his father worked for the military. But just a year into his life, Hillenburg's parents moved to Orange, California, nestled along the coast of the Pacific Ocean. His mother worked with visually impaired students and his father as a designer, often sitting for hours on end at a drafting table. They were both early influences on Stephen's desire to pick up a pencil and draw.

Television, another huge influence in Stephen's life, introduced the youngster to French oceanographer Jacques Cousteau, about whom we learn more and see a tribute to in the very first episode of *SpongeBob SquarePants*. Cousteau's documentaries about the sea, which were virtual windows beneath the waves, opened up a new world for Stephen Hillenburg—a world to which he would eventually bring his own special array of talents to share with us all.

In 1984, at the age of twenty-two, Hillenburg began working at the Ocean Institute in Dana Point, California, which runs educational programs for schoolkids. That's where the budding artist developed a comic book called *The Intertidal Zone*, about a tidal pool inhabited by tiny sea creatures. One of those creatures was Bob the Sponge.

How closely did that initial character resemble the SpongeBob we know today? Not much. Hillenburg modeled his original rendering on the type of sponge you would find in the ocean, classified scientifically as an organless Porifera. Round and puffy, it wore a pair of sunglasses, which the artist added for the coolness factor. Of course, the character didn't need pants, mainly because it didn't have any legs.

Upon returning to school to study art and animation at the California Institute of the Arts, Hillenburg made a pair of short animated films. *The Green Beret* (1991) is about a physically challenged Girl Scout with enormous fists who accidentally toppled entire neighborhoods while attempting to sell cookies door to door. *Wormholes* (1992), a Salvador Dali–esque glimpse at time and space from multiple perspectives, features a well-rounded world that's *almost* like ours.

Hillenburg's work caught the eye of the production team for a cartoon series called *Rocko's Modern Life* (1993–1996), and by 1993, he was actually working on that show for Nickelodeon.

During this period, Hillenburg focused on pitching his tidal pool characters to Nickelodeon as an animated show. SpongeBob (though that wasn't the character's name yet) was now square, reflecting both his personality and the shape of a household sponge you might find in the kitchen or bathroom. The addition of pants? Hillenburg believed that giving his protagonist pants would prevent potential viewers from mistaking the yellow, rectangular character for a piece of cheese. Consider the alternative possibilities: *CheddarBob*, *MozzarellaBob*, or perhaps even *StringCheese SquarePants*. Luckily, that never occurred.

An animated SpongeBob was introduced to the world on May 1, 1999, when Nickelodeon broadcast a preview of the series *SpongeBob SquarePants* directly after its highly rated *Kids' Choice Awards* show.

Then on July 17, the series made its official network debut, introducing viewers to the fun-loving, silly, and endearing undersea inhabitants of Bikini Bottom.

Note: The original May broadcast occurred just ten days after twelve students and one teacher lost their lives in the school shooting and attempted bombing of Columbine High School in Columbine, Colorado. Perhaps SpongeBob gave the country a needed smile during an extremely difficult time.

I–M–A–G–I–N–A–T–I–O–N

Just imagine you were an executive at Nickelodeon sitting in a conference room after Stephen Hillenburg made his pitch to get *SpongeBob* on the air. What would have been the chatter among your peers about the show's possibilities? Perhaps the conversation would have gone something like this: *"Well, from what I gather, he's a talking sponge. A real goody-goody*

A family experiencing the same type of awe that inspired Stephen Hillenburg.
Getty/shalamov

type. He's square, so he needs to wear square pants. After all, we can't put a naked sponge on TV. And his one ambition in life is to become a fry cook and wield a spatula. That's something new in kids' TV programming."

Now, be honest, would you have pounded your fist on the oversized table and proclaimed, "This character can't miss! He'll find his way into the hearts of millions!"?

HI, I'M SPONGEBOB

Our introduction to SpongeBob occurs in the very first episode, titled "Help Wanted," with him at home in his pineapple. Yes, I said "pineapple." We dive deeper into that later. He's fast asleep in bed and snoring loudly, about to be awakened by an alarm clock. What time is it? That's an interesting question. Hillenburg immediately lets us know that although Bikini Bottom mirrors our own society in many ways, there are some fun and subtle differences. For instance, the alarm clock has just eight numbers on its face instead of twelve. And Gary, SpongeBob's pet snail, *meows* like a cat. Fascinating.

SpongeBob is full of self-esteem. *Paramount/Photofest © Paramount Pictures*

A huge ship's horn attached to the alarm clock blows the blanket off our main character, who sleeps in his tighty-whities. That's right. Mr. SquarePants has square underwear too. No grumpy grogginess for SpongeBob. He bounces out of bed with childlike enthusiasm and climbs to the top of a tall indoor diving board.

"Today is the big day, Gary," SpongeBob informs both Gary and us.

He leaps off the board and out of his tighty-whities.

"Look at me! I'm naked!" proclaims SpongeBob.

Before we catch sight of SpongeBob in his full yellowness, he lands directly into his waiting square pants, complete with a square white shirt and a red tie. A tie? Well, this *is* a big day. In future episodes, we discover that every day in the life of SpongeBob is a big one, and the tie becomes a staple of his dress code.

This diving sequence, though, does leave discerning minds wondering. Was another pair of underwear already in those pants? Or does SpongeBob go commando during the day? During the course of the series, we discover that SpongeBob does in fact wear underwear during the day, sometimes multiple pairs and colors for comic effect.

SpongeBob exits his home and starts to chant what will become his inspirational mantra: "I'm ready! I'm ready!"

Not far down the road stands his fixation, an undersea fast-food restaurant. Immediately, SpongeBob lets us know that he has the soul of a poet. Well, sort of. "There it is," he muses. "The finest eating establishment ever established for eating. The Krusty Krab. Home of the krabby patty. With a help-wanted sign in the window."

But like most of us, SpongeBob suffers from self-doubt. Could his dream of slinging krabby patties as a fry cook be about to evaporate, even underwater?

"Don't you see? I'm not good enough," bemoans SpongeBob to his friend and neighbor Patrick Star, who lives under a rock, literally.

That's when the simplistic starfish shines as an exemplary friend, reminding our protagonist, "Whose first words were, 'May I take your order?' Who made a spatula out of toothpicks in woodshop? . . . And who's ready?"

"I'm ready!" responds a rejuvenated SpongeBob.

Entering the Krusty Krab, we meet Squidward Tentacles, a smug, high-brow octopus who works the register there. Squidward is another of SpongeBob's neighbors, and the pessimistic cephalopod (a class of species that includes octopus, squid, and cuttlefish) doesn't want anything to do with this naturally enthusiastic job applicant. Enter Mr. Krabs—the eatery's money-loving owner—who slyly sends SpongeBob on a quest for a turbo-driven, hydro-dynamic spatula with port and starboard ("port" is the left side of a ship and "starboard" is the right) attachments.

Squidward and Mr. Krabs enjoy a hearty laugh at SpongeBob's expense as our protagonist leaves in search of that mythical cooking implement. Where would SpongeBob find such a cooking tool? Why, at the Barg'N-Mart, naturally. It's Bikini Bottom's local supermarket and catchall (a fishing pun) shopping experience. The store is perfectly shaped like a pirate's treasure chest and even sports the skull and crossbones of the Jolly Roger, exactly something you might imagine that has sunken to the ocean floor.

During SpongeBob's absence, the Krusty Krab is besieged by a scourge of the sea, several busloads of hungry and smelly anchovies that overrun the restaurant like patty-starved zombies. Squidward and Mr. Krabs are forced to climb the Krusty Krab's crow's nest (a lookout platform high above a ship) as the waves of anchovies rock the restaurant like an angry tide.

Eventually, SpongeBob returns to save the day. He sails above the throngs of anchovies, propelled by the mythical spatula that he had been quested to find, most likely in the spatula aisle at Barg'N-Mart, where else? Entering the kitchen, our mild-mannered hero produces krabby patties at a supersonic rate, feeding the famished hordes. With their appetites now satisfied, the smelly anchovies board their buses and leave.

"That was the finest fast-foodsmanship I've ever seen, Mr. SquarePants. Welcome aboard!" proclaims Mr. Krabs, rewarding SpongeBob with his own Krusty Krab name tag, much to Squidward's dismay.

It is an episode that earns SpongeBob his life's ambition—the coveted title of "fry cook"—and sets the stage for the boundless fun to come in future episodes.

PERSPECTIVE: TOM KENNY

Tom Kenny, the voice of SpongeBob, was gracious enough to be interviewed for this book. He shares his perspective on many aspects of the series throughout the book.[1]

Q: Can you tell us about Stephen Hillenburg, who sadly passed away in late 2018? By all accounts, he was a terrific human being and an absolute creative force.

TK: Stephen Hillenburg was a total inspiration to me. That's because he was this purely creative person. He just wanted to create. *SpongeBob* would turn out to have really long legs; no one would have initially dreamed it could go on this long and make this big an impact. But I'm convinced that if Stephen hadn't sold the *SpongeBob* pilot, he would have gone back to his painting and animation and been just as happy.

Stephen was also very opinionated about the show and almost always absolutely correct about what was best for it. He was creating art for art's sake. He never devised a flowchart about what made other shows successful. He never tried to distill those characteristics down and put his own spin on it. He just made things up, and he made SpongeBob out of his passions and interests in life: art, drawing, music, characters, and a bunch of silly stuff that made him smile.

RECOGNIZING A LEGEND

Who is the first character to speak in the *SpongeBob SquarePants* series? Surprisingly, it isn't SpongeBob, though that first voice is indeed supplied by actor/comedian Tom Kenny, who also voices our beloved sponge. Instead, Kenny speaks to us as the narrator, performing a spot-on parody of famed oceanographer and environmentalist Jacques Cousteau (1910–1997).

"Ah, the sea, so fascinating . . . teeming with life. Home to one of my favorite creatures, SpongeBob SquarePants," says Kenny in a Cousteau-like French accent. "Yes. Of course, he lives in a pineapple, *you silly*."

If you're a teen or preteen and are not familiar with Cousteau's incredible exploits, that's quite understandable. Cousteau was the host of a popular documentary TV series called *The Undersea World of Jacques Cousteau* (1966–1976) and *The Cousteau Odyssey* (1977–1982). He dove the ocean's depths himself to record the beauty of all types of undersea life from aboard his ship, the *Calypso*, and was greatly admired by SpongeBob creator Stephen Hillenburg. Cousteau was even the coinventor of the Aqua Lung, the early forerunner of the scuba equipment used by divers today. And if the ocean truly had a voice, many people believe it would be that of Cousteau.

BUDDING RELATIONSHIPS

The opening episode concludes with a pair of segments that begin to explore SpongeBob's relationships with others. In "Reef Blowers," which focuses on the neighborly strife between SpongeBob and Squidward (with all the strife resting upon Squidward's huge forehead), the pair compete for the cleanest yard, attempting to push a lone clamshell onto the other's property.

Neither character speaks throughout this segment, with a soundtrack of background music and SpongeBob's noisy reef blower, an undersea version of our leaf blowers. The ensuing action is cartoon slapstick—a type of physical comedy at its best—leaving Squidward buried beneath a huge pile of sand. It's a signal to the audience that Squidward's sour nature is probably never going to triumph over SpongeBob's persistent cheerfulness.

In "Tea at the Tree Dome," SpongeBob, who is out jellyfishing (though the activity isn't yet named), encounters Sandy Cheeks for the first time. "Where have I seen this before?" ponders SpongeBob, producing a field guide of animal species. "Here it is. Land squirrel." Does this mean that SpongeBob has previously been to the surface world?

SpongeBob and Sandy instantly bond over their love of karate, or, as they call it, *ka-rah-tay*. Sandy, who wears an air helmet for oxygen, invites our protagonist to her home for tea. After accepting, SpongeBob sprints to Patrick Star's rock to ask, "Patrick, what's air? I just met this girl. She wears a hat full of air."

"Do you mean she puts on airs?" responds the starfish in a moment reminiscent of a *Dumb and Dumber* vocabulary quiz. "That's just fancy talk. If you want to be fancy, hold your pinkie up like this. The higher you hold it, the fancier you are."

Of course, Patrick has no fingers and SpongeBob has just four digits. But for a moment, they each manage to magically hold up a pinkie.

Sandy lives in a treedome, which is void of water and filled with air. After several minutes visiting there, SpongeBob and Patrick, who rushes inside to save his friend, dry out. When Sandy, who had excused herself to fetch the tea, returns, she is horrified by the sight of a real-life dehydrated kitchen sponge and a rigid starfish—like the ones found in curio shops—lying prone on the ground. The instant remedy: a helmet like hers, but filled with water (and steeping tea), instead of air, for her guests.

BENEATH THE SURFACE

Stephen Hillenburg wasn't one to moralize in his stories or to tell viewers how to think or feel. He trusted in the writing and the characters to make an impression on the viewers. But every so often, we take a closer look at Hillenburg's episodes and talk about what we see. You'll undoubtedly have opinions of your own. Comparing viewpoints is what makes discussing art so special.

In "Tea at the Treedome," the inclusion of Sandy, an air breather, subtly adds to the diversity of Bikini Bottom. That's something Hillenburg and the writing staff achieve in many different fashions during the course of the series. Sandy also gives us our first female perspective, something vitally important in reflecting who we truly are as a society onto this underwater community.

BART SIMPSON AND SPONGEBOB?

Within the first minute of our introduction to Sponge-Bob SquarePants, he proclaims, "I'm naked!" It seems our oh-so-good protagonist has the same penchant for nudity in common with the devilish Bart Simpson. We were introduced to Bart's bare butt before *The Simpsons* (1989–present) had their own show. In four of the short vignettes that appeared on *The Tracey Ullman Show* (1987–1990), Bart found the need to get naked for us.

When the dysfunctional family was given its own primetime platform, it didn't take long for Bart to shed his trademark red t-shirt and blue shorts. During the premiere season's second episode, titled "Bart the Genius," we catch a glimpse of a naked Bart, whose skin turned green in a failed school science experiment.

Naturally, no fleeting glimpse compares to Bart's one-minute-plus naked skateboard ride through the heart of Springfield in *The Simpsons Movie* (2007), in which items such as an old woman's pointing finger, a dove in flight, a leaf from a bush, and a French fry held by Ned Flanders block his privates from view.

QUIZ QUESTION 1

What is SpongeBob's middle name? *Hint:* He clearly informs Sandy of this upon their initial meeting; however, since he's trying to impress her, it may not be exactly what is on his birth certificate. Wait, did I just say that a sponge has a birth certificate?

The answer can be found after the book's conclusion.

2

BECOMING SPONGEBOB

FROM "BOY" TO "BOB"

The character we know and love as SpongeBob SquarePants wasn't always who he is today. In fact, he wasn't even named SpongeBob, nor did he bear the name of his earlier incarnation, Bob the Sponge. The character was named Sponge Boy, and the series that Stephen Hillenburg originally pitched to Nickelodeon was titled *Sponge Boy Ahoy!* So what happened? Well, Nick's legal department believed that name already had a copyright owned by another entity, so the change was made to SpongeBob.

During Hillenburg's presentation to network executives—one in which he played Hawaiian music in the background, wore a colorful Hawaiian shirt (mirroring the eventual concept for Bikini Bottom's underwater "sky" filled with sea flowers), and displayed models of the characters in an underwater terrarium—those in attendance received what is known as a pitch bible, explaining both the characters and series concept.

It was in that pitch bible, complete with drawings and future story ideas, that Hillenburg first described his yellow, absorbent, porous hero. "An undersea cartoon starring the world's most rectangular [off-beat character], Sponge Boy! . . . He's a single male sponge who resides in a fully furnished, two bedroom . . . pineapple. He has an abnormal love for his job at 'The Crusty Crab' [spelled with *C*s at the time, not *K*s], a fast-food restaurant. In fact, he's so proud of his Crusty Crab uniform that he never takes it off, not even when he showers."[1]

What would ultimately set Hillenburg's protagonist apart from the normal cartoonish fare of do-gooders and wise-cracking characters aimed at children and adolescents? Despite a treasure chest of positive characteristics, including being kind, loyal, and incurably optimistic, Sponge-Bob never seems to completely fit in to this undersea society, which often mirrors our own. His unconventional, well-meaning approach to almost every situation causes conflict, mostly for others. This likable underdog who embraces every moment regularly sets comic chaos into motion through his actions.

"Sponge Boy would like to fit in," notes Hillenburg in his pitch bible. "His ideal is to be like everyone else. He wants to buy into that dream of 'service with a smile,' and be that team player, that company man with the positive mental attitude. But he never quite attains this goal, and, more importantly, he will never recognize this fact. Here we discover the tragic side of Sponge Boy. Don't get nervous! He is tragic to some extent. . . . We see Sponge Boy as built from within, observing that, this creates sympathies and qualities which resonate. His desire to fit in, combined with his innocence about his inability to do so, creates conflict."

Of course, Nickelodeon significantly influenced the evolving character. Before the series was picked up as the network's first original Saturday morning cartoon, Hillenburg had to agree to find a way to get SpongeBob into school. Why? Nick had incredible success with characters who shared that trait with—and thus were more relatable to—its school-age audience. Hence, post–pitch bible, Hillenburg created the character of Mrs. Puff, owner of a boating school. SpongeBob takes her class, creating storylines about his seemingly never-ending attempts at getting a boating license.

So they drive boats *underwater*? Forget it. Just go with the flow!

SURF'S UP!

Early episodes focus on fleshing out the character of SpongeBob (although he's made of sponge, not skin), his relationships, and the world in which he lives. What do the sea creatures of Bikini Bottom do for fun? In the episode "Ripped Pants" (season 1, episode 2), they go to an underwater beach and even get sunburned. The beach is called Goo Lagoon, a not-so-subtle homage to both Iceland's famed Blue Lagoon and the 1980 film *Blue Lagoon*, about a pair of preteens shipwrecked alone in the South Pacific. Goo Lagoon is described by the narrator as "a stinky mud puddle to you and me. But to the inhabitants of Bikini Bottom, a *wonderful* stinky mud puddle."

SpongeBob is definitely smitten with Sandy and tries to impress her in every possible way as they sit beneath the same beach umbrella along the crowded shore. In his pitch bible, Hillenburg even refers to their outings together as "dates." Not the romantic kind, mind you. But rather the type in which one of the characters might break a limb and require cartoon traction.

Our yellow protagonist goes green with jealousy when the buff Larry the Lobster and Sandy compete at beach sports such as volleyball and Frisbee. SpongeBob can neither keep up with the pair nor hold Sandy's attention. When SpongeBob accidentally rips his pants while lifting weights (actually two marshmallows attached to either end of a stick) on the beach, he gets a big laugh and everyone's attention. As the day wears on, craving that public attention again, he tries to be part of the cool "in crowd." Annoyingly, he replays that physical pants-splitting gag over and over until he eventually loses the crowd's favor.

In a last-ditch effort to regain that thrillingly short-lived popularity, he pretends to be drowning after wiping out while surfing. A lifeguard (apparently sea creatures can flounder in the water and need protection) first mistakes SpongeBob for a cardboard box that washed up with tide—at least our protagonist wasn't mistaken for a block of cheese—then rushes to rescue him.

"What do you need?" the concerned lifeguard asks, cradling the seemingly lifeless sponge in his arms.

"A tailor," whispers SpongeBob before suddenly snapping back to life. "Because I ripped my pants!"

It's one of the rare scenes in the series in which SpongeBob comes off looking like an insensitive dolt. Everyone, including Sandy, turns their backs in disappointment on SpongeBob. That's when a stray sea creature tells him, "If you want to be my friend, just be yourself."

Left alone, SpongeBob reflects on his attention-seeking prank. He then forms an impromptu musical band with other so-called losers and sings an apologetic song on the beach—fittingly a parody of a Beach Boys tune—vocalizing that he learned a valuable lesson. It's a toe-tapping, hip-swaying apology that his friends accept.

BENEATH THE SURFACE

Hillenburg shows us that SpongeBob wants to be liked and loved—and sometimes the center of attention. "Ripped Pants" proves to viewers that SpongeBob has the same needs and self-doubts that we all do. The episode also marks the beginning of Hillenburg's use of song to connect emotions, character, and plot in the series—something he soon learns to master—giving us some of SpongeBob's most memorable and endearing musical moments.

COINING A PHRASE

Stephen Hillenburg and the writers of *SpongeBob SquarePants* unknowingly added to our lexicon of pleasant pastimes when they titled an early episode "Jellyfishing" (season 1, episode 3).

Jellyfish buzz past SpongeBob's pineapple like our garden-variety bees in search of pollen to make honey. Except that Bikini Bottom's jellyfish make, well, jelly. Where can they be found congregating? Jellyfish Fields, naturally.

SpongeBob and Patrick, in true Batman-and-Robin form, ready themselves for action to dramatic background music, taking the pineapple's inner passages to a secret room where they arm themselves with long-handled nets. SpongeBob even snaps on a pair of thick safety glasses. Can't be too careful when it comes to being safe.

Are the duo about to confront some denizen of the deep? A menacing sea monster wreaking total havoc? No. They're going "jellyfishing."

As the dramatic music concludes, a jellyfish softly buzzes by and our protagonists skip after it in not-so-hot pursuit, singing, "La-la-la-la-la."

Wait. Bees can sting. Can jellyfish sting, too? They can. And our less-than-dynamic duo get chased back to the pineapple by a cute baby jellyfish that comically zaps both of their behinds.

Enter Squidward, who wants nothing more than to ride his bicycle (equipped with water paddles instead of wheels) on a calm and beautiful morning.

"Hey, Squidward. We're jellyfishing," says SpongeBob.

"Of course you are," replies Squidward in a dismissive tone, pushing his bicycle away.

But the pair made a net especially for Squidward, and they want him to join them.

Squidward's forthcoming speech is lathered in sarcasm, which neither simpleton recognizes. "Really? Jellyfishing with you guys. That would be the best day ever in my book. . . . I can't think of anything I'd rather do on my day off than go jellyfishing with my two best friends SpongeBob and . . . " hesitates Squidward, seemingly not knowing Patrick's name.

As Squidward rides off, Patrick wonders, "Maybe he doesn't like us."

"Are you kidding?" counters SpongeBob. "We're his best friends."

A stray jellyfish causes Squidward to ride his bike off a steep cliff, resulting in serious cartoon injury (a wheelchair and bandages). Apparently, where cliffs are concerned, gravity applies underwater the way it

Stephen Hillenburg and SpongeBob coined the phrase "jellyfishing." *Nickelodeon/Photofest*
© *Nickelodeon*

does on the surface. And Bikini Bottom has a hospital of some sort, in which Squidward endures an extended stay.

Upon his return home, the clueless pair take the helpless Squidward—who can't protest because his mouth is bandaged shut—jellyfishing. That's where the wheelchair-bound Squidward encounters the mother of all jellyfish—one large enough to cast a shadow completely over him.

"This guy's good!" says Patrick of Squidward's prowess.

"He's a natural!" concludes SpongeBob from a safe distance.

But the ominous music lets us know exactly what's coming in the end for Squidward—*Zap!*

SCRIPT BLUNDER?

In the opening episode of the series, Squidward calls Patrick by name when the starfish orders food at the Krusty Krab. Did he really forget Patrick's name by the third episode? Did the show's writers simply forget that Squidward had already used the name? Or did Squidward draw a blank for effect to let the audience know that he didn't desire Patrick's friendship?

What do you think?

QUIZ QUESTION 2

At the welcome-home celebration for the wheelchair-bound Squidward in "Jellyfishing," SpongeBob joyously screams, "Welcome Home!" Patrick Star's greeting is incongruous but tells us that holidays are also celebrated in Bikini Bottom. Do you recall what Patrick says?

The answer can be found after the book's conclusion.

A PINEAPPLE HOME?

The pineapple (*Ananas comosus*) is a flowering tropical plant with edible fruit that grows on a small shrublike bush. Though it's indigenous to South America, Christopher Columbus brought it back to Europe, where it became a symbol of wealth due to the cost it took to import there or to grow in greenhouses.

But how could SpongeBob have wound up living in one?

Today, the Philippines and Indonesia, a pair of island nations bordered by the Pacific Ocean, are among the world leaders in the production of pineapples. Did Stephen Hillenburg imagine that one fell off a ship during transport? But wait a minute—don't pineapples float? They certainly do. And some pineapple connoisseurs contend that the riper ones float higher in the water.

So why is SpongeBob's healthy-looking pineapple sitting at the bottom of the ocean?

Sometimes it's best to accept things the way they're presented. You don't dissect gossamer (a delicate fabric or silky webbing). And that may be the best way to describe the inner workings of Hillenburg's fertile imagination.

By the way, several of the furnishings inside of SpongeBob's pineapple home—including a wall-mounted fishing lure and fishhooks used as table legs—reflect Hillenburg's salvage-minded vision for Bikini Bottom—something we explore in greater depth later in a section called "Recycle City."

FAN FORUM

Here's the first installment of a recurring section revealing what fans around the country think about the series.

"SpongeBob has always held a special place in my heart. Early mornings or late nights, it didn't matter, I would watch. . . . SpongeBob helped me through childhood and opened up new ideas or solutions to problems relating to the outside world. I think the show's humor can make anyone smile, especially me."—K. C.

3

THE THEME SONG

I CAN HEAR IT!

What opens every episode of *SpongeBob SquarePants*? Undoubtedly one of the most popular and catchiest theme songs to ever start a TV show—whether you love or hate the fact that you can't get it out of your mind. The music to the theme song was written by Mark Harrison and Blasie Smith, while series creator Stephen Hillenburg and creative director Derek Drymon penned the lyrics.

"Are you ready, kids?" asks Painty the Pirate before the song kicks into gear.

Exactly who is Painty the Pirate? He is a pirate or buccaneer in a framed painting that Stephen Hillenburg found in a thrift shop. Voice actor Patrick Piney sings Painty's part, but the live-action lips superimposed over those in the painting actually belong to Hillenburg, in one of the audience's rare glimpses of him.

The theme song is a classic example of call-and-response, often used in musical styles such as blues, gospel, and even hip-hop. The leader—in this case Painty—calls to the audience for a response. "Aye, aye, Captain," the kids—viewers—affirm by responding. Call-and-response has its roots in African culture, where it is used in public gatherings, religious rituals, and musical expressions.

The high-energy theme song lasts just forty-three seconds. But in that short period of time, we hear the main character's full name, SpongeBob SquarePants, shouted a remarkable eight times. The song also foreshadows something the series does amazingly well—mixing the features of real-life, live-action images with animation. Our first glimpse of SpongeBob, at his pineapple door, is in his tighty-whities. That is, until a cardboard cutout of a real arm, clothed in what appears to be a naval captain's uniform, hangs a pair of square pants on the character's lower half. Listeners also hear some snappy alliteration in the rhyme scheme, including "nautical nonsense," "drop on the deck," and "flop like a fish."

As an original drawing of Sponge Boy fills the screen, SpongeBob rises into view, blocking that image and leading the music out by playing the theme's final notes on his nose, as if it were a flute.

NO LANGUAGE BARRIER HERE

There are approximately forty versions of the song made for the various languages into which the *SpongeBob SquarePants* series has been translated. Want to learn a new language? You can start by listening to this song, which you probably know word-for-word, in other tongues. These other languages include Arabic, Brazilian Portuguese, Greek, Hebrew, Hungarian, French, Icelandic, Serbian, Slovenian, and Ukrainian. In Dutch, the theme song opens with the call, *"Kunnen we, kinderen?"* And the response being, *"Aye-aye, Kapitein!"* It is recognized in Italy as, *"Siete pronti, ragazzi."* With the kids answering, *"Si, signor Capitano."*

ALT BOB

In *The SpongeBob SquarePants Movie* (2004), Canadian-born singer and songwriter Avril Lavigne lays down the track for a hard-rocking alternative version of the theme song in which she sings both the call and response parts. "I made the song a little more edgy," Lavigne told MTV. "It's kind of like the rock version of [the original]. There are a lot of loud guitars, and we picked the tempo up a little and sang it with a little more attitude."[1]

By the way, "Avril" is French word for the month of April. Avril Lavigne, however, was born in September. Go figure!

PARODIES

A parody is an imitation of something extremely recognizable, either done to praise or poke fun at the well-known version. The *SpongeBob SquarePants* theme song has been parodied many times. When McDonald's distributed SpongeBob toys with their Happy Meals in 2012, the world's most famous fast-food chain (sorry, Krusty Krab) decided to use a parody of the theme in its commercials. Did Mickey D's mention burgers, krabby patties, or fries in the revised song lyrics? No. Instead, in an era of more health-conscious consumers, the chain wisely focused on the fact that milk and fruit came with the meal.

The series has been known to poke fun at itself. In a trio of silly parodies in the episode "Unreal Estate" (season 10, episode 2), Squidward, hoping to make his annoyingly pleasant neighbor move, tries to convince the trusting sponge that he has become allergic to the pineapple in which he resides. As Squidward brings SpongeBob to other oddly shaped Bikini Bottom abodes, the theme song's opening is rewritten and played during the episode to reflect each possible new home. "Who lives in a banana under the sea?" "Who lives in a hot pepper under the sea?" And perhaps the silliest of all, "Who lives in a chicken parmesan gyro under the sea?"

BASEBALL WALK-UP MUSIC

For many baseball players and fans, it was an extremely tense moment. The Cleveland Guardians were batting in the bottom of the fifteenth inning in a still-scoreless Major League Baseball playoff game against the Tampa Bay Rays on October 8, 2022. One person not experiencing that pressure, however, was Cleveland's rookie outfielder Oscar Gonzalez, a native of the Dominican Republic. Gonzalez happens to be a huge fan of *SpongeBob SquarePants*. So much so that Gonzalez uses the show's theme song as his walk-up music, which is played at the Guardians' home stadium, Progressive Field, whenever he strides to the plate for his turn at bat.

"[I chose it] because kids love that song and this is a kid's game after all," said the twenty-four-year-old Gonzalez.[2]

With strains of "Who lives in a pineapple under the sea? SpongeBob SquarePants!" echoing through the sold-out stadium, Gonzalez delivered a massive solo home run to win the game 1 to 0 and to advance the Guardians further into the playoffs. As the outfielder rounded the bases, more than thirty-five thousand fans in attendance raised their voices to serenade Gonzalez with the theme. That's one way to keep the high-pressure world of professional sports fun.

"I walk to the plate singing along with the song. It reminds me that even though I have a big body, deep inside I feel like a little kid."[3]

QUIZ QUESTION 3

The *SpongeBob SquarePants* theme song begins and concludes with the sounds of what animals?

The answer can be found after the book's conclusion.

THE FIRST
TEN EPISODES

CHARACTER BUILDING

Throughout the episodes that mark the halfway point of the first *season* (that's underwater humor), Stephen Hillenburg continued to shade in the daily lives of his colorful characters and their personalities. In "Naughty Nautical Neighbors" (season 1, episode 4), we glimpse the soufflé-cooking Squidward wearing an apron that reads, "Kiss the Squid!" It's a subtle bit of fun aimed at an audience still coming to grips with an octopus named Squidward.

We learn that despite his perpetual good humor, every now and then even SpongeBob's frustration builds to the point where the language he uses reflects his anger. His less-than-cheery go-to phrase, later repeated by Patrick, is simply, "Awe, tartar sauce!" It's an interesting choice of words considering that tartar sauce often accompanies seafood meals.

SpongeBob shows his compulsive side in "Hall Monitor" (season 1, episode 7) when it's his turn to take that post for the day in boating school.

"I'm ready to assume my position, in the hall. I will protect all that are weak, in the hall. All rules will be enforced, in the hall," says the overly committed SpongeBob, who isn't ready to put on the hall monitor's uniform (a belt and hat) until he makes a formal acceptance speech. "Friends, students, juvenile delinquents—lend me your ears."

But by the time his speech has concluded, boating school is over for the day.

"I overdid the speech again, didn't I?" he admits with a bit of self-realization.

I-M-A-G-I-N-A-T-I-O-N

"Naughty Nautical Neighbors" also features "whisper bubbles." It seems that if you whisper words of friendship into a bubble wand before blowing a bubble, your whispered message can be heard when that bubble eventually pops beside your best friend. It's a wonderfully imaginative idea developed by Hillenburg and the writing team, perfectly befitting the childlike personalities of SpongeBob and Patrick. That pair trade wonderful pleasantries via bubbles until Squidward intervenes. He spoils their good time by sending them bubbles, supposedly from each other, with less-than-flattering messages attached.

"If I had a dollar for every brain you don't have, I'd have one dollar," echoes Squidward's disguised voice in a mean-spirited bubble message.

It's a case of imaginary communication gone haywire. Perhaps an early vision of catfishing (how appropriate) meant to break up good friends. Don't worry. Squidward gets his just desserts when the now divided pair begin to fight over him, each claiming that he's their best friend. Not quite what Squidward had in mind.

BENEATH THE SURFACE

Squidward is so stuck-up that Stephen Hillenburg eventually needs to prove to us that the character has some redeeming qualities as well. That moment arrives in "Pizza Delivery" (season 1, episode 5), after Mr. Krabs quickly fashions a delivery pizza for a shell-phone customer who doesn't want a krabby patty. Question: Does deep-sea pizza come with anchovies as a topping, or is that simply in bad taste?

SpongeBob and Squidward are tasked with making the pizza delivery. After getting lost and becoming stranded, the pair finally arrive at the address. Their pepperoni and cheese odyssey seems complete until the rude customer refuses to accept delivery because they've forgotten his drink, a Diet Dr. Kelp (Dr. Pepper?), causing SpongeBob to cry uncontrollably.

A moment later, Squidward, who won't allow his friend to be mistreated in such a fashion, knocks on the door alone and delivers the pizza in the way that rude customer has coming—*pow!*

"He ate the whole thing in one bite," Squidward assures the concerned SpongeBob.

It's an ending that redeems, at least for the moment, the somewhat dislikeable Squidward.

PERSPECTIVE: TOM KENNY

Q: It seems that the show's amazing characters often overwhelm the idea of plot in a given episode.

TK: Characters were always more important to Stephen Hillenburg than plot, and he was absolutely correct in his thinking. It's the characters that find a home in our collective consciousness. It's more about who they are than what they do. I call it "personality over plot." Stephen had the essence of these characters—SpongeBob, Patrick, Squidward, Mr. Krabs, Sandy, and Pearl—ready to roll before he ever pitched the idea of a show starring SpongeBob to a living soul. It had all been gestating in his brain for years while he was a camp counselor, marine biologist, and, finally, studying animation.

ADDED FOUNDATION

Bikini Bottom boasts a police force, a jail, and a fire department. Fires underwater? Yup. Extinguished by hero, civil-servant fish. Still unbalanced by the incongruity? Take Tom Kenny's advice: "Just don't ask about it, and let it go."

During these early episodes, we learn that SpongeBob keeps a diary and that Patrick has no qualms about reading it when his best friend isn't around. In fact, Patrick seems to respect few social boundaries.

"What's pink and square at the same time?" Patrick asks the absent SpongeBob while rummaging through his possessions at the pineapple.

The answer?

"Patrick SquarePants," laughs the starfish, jamming his oversized body into a pair of his friend's pants without permission.

We're also introduced to a number of characters that give greater depth, foundation, and fun to SpongeBob's life. Mrs. Puff has been our protagonist's frustrated boating instructor for semester after semester. Aged undersea superheroes Mermaid Man and Barnacle Boy, who are currently residents in a rest home, are the subject of hero worship by SpongeBob and Patrick. The tiny Plankton is focused on stealing the krabby patty recipe from the Krusty Krab, which he hopes will ultimately lead to him ruling the world. And SpongeBob's parents, Mr. and Mrs. SquarePants, who live beyond the borders of Bikini Bottom, have rounded, true-to-life sponge heads, unlike their perfectly square son.

Our main tour guide in this submerged society is the creative mind of Stephen Hillenburg. Linking Bikini Bottom to our surface world isn't always easy, but he was consistently on target.

In "Squeaky Boots" (season 1, episode 8), Hillenburg parodies the work of Edgar Allan Poe's *The Tell-Tale Heart* with a comedic twist that's tightly laced with both mystery and macabre (typically horrifying by its relation to death or injury). The setup? Mr. Krabs bamboozles SpongeBob into accepting a pair of old boots that supposedly belonged to a famed fry cook instead of his paycheck. But his conscience gets the best of him as the squeaking of SpongeBob walking in those boots overwhelms every other sound. Haunted by the squeaks, Mr. Krabs eventually steals the boots and hides them beneath the floorboards of the Krusty Krab, mirroring Poe's story.

On the verge of losing his mind, Mr. Krabs is forced to set things right to regain his sanity. Exactly how does he do that? Why, Mr. Krabs eats the boots after deep-frying them. What else would a fast-food proprietor do? Naturally, he gives SpongeBob his paycheck, too.

BIKINI BOTTOM

HISTORICAL SIGNIFICANCE

Stephen Hillenburg didn't pull the name Bikini Bottom out of thin air, though on the surface, it sounds like a rather cheeky and comical place. But in his pitch bible, Hillenburg makes it clear that Bikini Bottom is submerged beneath the real-life Bikini Atoll, a coral reef in the Pacific Ocean's Marshall Islands, consisting of twenty-three islands that surround a nearly 230-square-mile lagoon.

"Where does Sponge Boy live? Why, in the ocean, of course!" said Hillenburg in his pitch bible for the show. "In the Pacific Ocean, actually, a few fathoms beneath the tropical Isle of Bikini Atoll, in the sub-surface city of Bikini Bottom."

Bikini Atoll has historical significance and an unfortunate history. After World War II (1939–1945), the native inhabitants there were, in essence, forcibly relocated from the place of their heritage, and Bikini Atoll became the site of twenty-three nuclear tests conducted by the United States. The beautiful necklace of coral islands became uninhabitable for the succeeding two decades due to the radiation that remained. Then,

One of the nuclear blasts that left Bikini Atoll uninhabitable for so many years.
Getty/Digital Vision

in 1970, many native families were allowed to return. But these reestablished islanders began to suffer serious health issues at an alarming rate, until the area was once again evacuated. Today, only a small contingent of scientists and caretakers reside there.

By choosing this particular site for his series, Hillenburg, a staunch environmentalist, keeps the name "Bikini Atoll" in our conversation. And his fertile imagination opens the door to an interesting parallel—an obvious notion of cause and effect. Is it possible that an underwater society complete with talking sponges, fish, crabs, and a clarinet-playing snooty octopus is a result of these nuclear tests?

Hillenburg created a fantastical backstory for his discovery of Bikini Bottom. His pitch bible includes the fictitious quest of a diver named Bucky Leavitt, who had hand drawn the only known map of Bikini Bottom. According to Hillenburg, the diver lost his life in 1947 when his diving suit buckled from the immense deep-sea pressure. A half-century later, though, Hillenburg and his team of explorers finished Leavitt's task of exploring Bikini Bottom.

"Eureka! The sense of epic discovery, that adrenaline-filled moment, like landing on the moon or uncovering the tomb of Tutankhamun—this is what every scientist dreams of. We were awestruck," wrote Hillenburg. "And as the veil of mystery surrounding the briny deep's funniest yellow cube lifted before our very eyes, we were afforded a first-hand glimpse into the character of Sponge Boy and his world. There before us, glistening in the glow of our dive lamps, sat a submerged treasure unlike any other in the world."

Bikini Bottom would turn out to be a lot like our surface world. And, therefore, ultimately relatable. Its citizens commute to work, wait in line at the movies, care for their pets, and celebrate holidays. Bikini Bottom's similarities and differences to our society tickle our funny bones and tug at our heartstrings.

The wonder of a diver examining a coral reef amid the beauty beneath Bikini Atoll. *Getty/moodboard*

EUREKA!

Stephen Hillenburg uses the word *eureka* in his pitch bible to punctuate his discovery of Bikini Bottom. The word comes from ancient Greek and translates as "I found [it]." Its usage is attributed to the Greek scholar Archimedes, who shouted, "Eureka!" after lowering himself into a tub of water, observing that the water level rose, and realizing that the volume of water displaced must be equal to the mass of his partially submerged body. Archimedes also is said to have been so excited by his discovery that he jumped out of the tub and ran naked through the streets, shouting about his insight. I guess SpongeBob isn't the only one who has trouble keeping his clothes on.

SpongeBob's creator actually misspelled the word in his pitch bible (spelling it Ureka!). Nickelodeon executives gave Hillenburg a passing grade anyway and picked up the series.

QUIZ QUESTION 4

A model of a small surface island, a fictitious representation of Bikini Atoll, is shown above Bikini Bottom at the start of the theme song and opening credits. Picture it in your mind. Exactly how many palm trees grow on that island?

The answer can be found after the book's conclusion.

RECYCLE CITY

From the audience's opening view of Bikini Bottom in the premiere episode of *SpongeBob SquarePants*, creator Stephen Hillenburg makes one thing absolutely clear about his underwater city: it mostly uses our refuse to create its physical structures. Old tin cans, anchors, boots, lobster traps, empty buckets, life preservers (how do they stay submerged?), a boat propeller, sunken ships, and other types of debris that find their way into this landscape undoubtedly are turned into homes or places of business by Bottomites.

It's a powerful statement for a marine biologist such as Hillenburg to make—keeping our oceans cleaner and turning its trash into something useful is important. In fact, a season seven episode titled "Keep Bikini Bottom Beautiful" (episode 13) wonderfully emphasizes this concept. While out for a walk, Squidward accidentally steps in chewing gum that has been carelessly tossed onto the ground. After comically extricating himself from its sticky nature, Squidward leaves it by the side of the road. But a police officer witnesses his action and confronts him.

"I just stepped in it," says Squidward.

"You sure did, buddy," responds the officer, writing Squidward a ticket for littering. "Maybe this will teach you not to treat the world as your own personal garbage can."

Squidward is sentenced to community service picking up roadside trash. He receives several more tickets for littering while trying to clean up. Then SpongeBob decides to help his friend and the neighborhood by pitching in. But after collecting a huge mound of trash, the pair discovers that the city dump is closed. So SpongeBob secretly does something incredibly positive with the trash. Squidward doesn't care what he's done with it, as long as he can go home to his Easter Island head and rest. But SpongeBob, in the spirit of Bikini Bottom, has built an exact replica of Squidward's home with the wayward trash. It takes a while for the self-absorbed Squidward, who unwittingly brushes his teeth with garbage, to notice that he's not in his original house. But eventually he does, and Hillenburg and the writing staff's point about what to do with the ocean's enormous pile of trash is beautifully made.

NOT IN BIKINI BOTTOM

When SpongeBob cleans up the Krusty Krab parking lot, he's not joking around. He dons a hat that reads "Litter Bugs Me." In "SpongeBob Meets the Strangler" (season 3, episode 20), our porous protagonist spots a repeat offender littering at will. The police actually show up and arrest the culprit. For littering? No, he's a wanted criminal named the Tattle-Tale Strangler, who now wants to get even with SpongeBob for turning him in. The Strangler escapes the authorities and returns in disguise (after buying a fake mustache at the mall's Phony Baloney Mustache Emporium) as a bodyguard for SpongeBob, safeguarding him from the Strangler's revenge. But over the course of the day, SpongeBob's nonstop niceness and naivete cause the Strangler to basically turn himself in, seeing jail as a reprieve.

Hey, buddy, don't litter in this town.

REAL-LIFE OCEAN POLLUTANTS

According to the National Geographic Society, the world's oceans are contaminated with approximately 5.25 trillion bits of plastic trash. Plastics, which comprise 90 percent of ocean debris, can have a devastating impact on marine life and ecosystems, including causing disease to coral reefs. Some of the worst offenders in this category are plastic bottle caps and straws. That's why there's a current push to switch from plastic straws to either paper or reusable metal ones. (SpongeBob's friend Bubble Buddy likes to use a bendy straw. I hope it's not the plastic type.)

There are just too many plastics polluting our oceans. *Getty/solarseven*

Too much plastic in the water can cause eutrophication, a process that increases the chemical nutrient concentration in a body of water. A byproduct of that process is lower oxygen levels in the water, creating dead zones with little to no marine life.

Heavy metals such as lead, cadmium, arsenic, and mercury also contaminate our oceans. Pesticides, phenols, and polychlorinated biphenyls, more commonly known as PCBs, also cause great harm. Some of the world's largest rivers, like the Nile (Africa) and the Ganges (Asia), are major contributors in delivering industrial pollutants into our oceans. There's even a stretch of densely polluted waterway referred to as the Great Pacific Garbage Patch, reaching from the western coast of the United States to Japan, where the surface trash can be viewed for miles and miles.

Part of Stephen Hillenburg's conception of Bikini Bottom, situated beneath the Pacific Ocean, is a reflection of these major ecological issues.

CELEBRATIONS AND AMUSEMENTS

The inhabitants of Bikini Bottom celebrate Christmas, April Fools' Day, Valentine's Day, birthdays (with party games such as pin the tail on the seahorse), and Halloween with costumed young ones trick-or-treating for candy.

The prize for the best Halloween costume in Bikini Bottom? It goes to Sandy, who transforms her air helmet into a fishbowl while adding gold-colored fins and scales to her head to make herself resemble a goldfish. It's a brilliant costume, but Squidward looks at her and says, "I don't get it." Could it be that these native aquatics have never seen an aquarium?

Squidward even invents his own holiday in "Opposite Day" (episode 9). It's an attempt to get his neighbors, SpongeBob and Patrick, to act normally (not like themselves), so he can sell his Easter Island head house and finally move.

"Opposite Day is the one day of the year when you get to act different," says Squidward. "Normally, I'm stuffy, boring"—it feels good to hear him finally admit it—"but today, I'm silly and spontaneous. . . . Normally you're loud and annoying, so what are you going to be today?"

"Quiet and out of the way!" screams SpongeBob at the top of his lungs.

Naturally, the plan totally backfires, as SpongeBob and Patrick try to become just like Squidward and ultimately convince the saleswoman from Bikini Realty that they're *both* him in a comic transformation.

Hey, shouldn't it be "Bikini *Un*-Realty"? After all, Bikini Bottom is fictitious.

Other distractions?

There are museums, board games, important teen dances like the junior prom, and carnivals with cotton candy and Ferris wheels. The Disney-inspired Glove World is a theme park where patrons wear gloves on their heads instead of mouse ears. Submarine-like buses serve as mass transportation to these fun spots, and the physical landmarks such as Jellyfish Fields and Mount Climb-up and Fall-off often serve as recreational outlets.

Other submerged communities surrounding Bikini Bottom include Ukulele Bottom, where a jellyfishing convention is held, and Rock Bottom, whose inhabitants punctuate their speech by sticking out their tongues and blowing a *pptth* sound in the middle of every word. *Say it, don't spray it, Rock Bottomites!*

GREAT NEPTUNE!

We also discover that there is a deity in Bikini Bottom when a regretful Squidward, who has forgotten his promise to feed Gary while snail-sitting during a long three-day weekend, says, "Oh, Neptune! What have I done?" In fact, lots of characters reference the powerful godlike being with remarks such as, "Merciful Neptune," "What in Neptune's name?" "Thank Neptune," and "Great Neptune in heaven." Only Neptune doesn't reside in heaven. Instead, he inhabits the otherworldly Atlantis, which magically appears via a portal whenever Neptune so decrees it.

Neptune is depicted by Stephen Hillenburg and the artists as an immense turquoise figure (Squidward will find some pride in that) with flowing red hair and beard, golden wristbands, and a matching trident. Oh, and he's an absolute jerk!

The audience gets their introduction to Neptune, voiced by John O'Hurley, whom you may remember as Mr. Peterman from the series *Seinfeld*, in "Neptune's Spatula" (episode 19).

SpongeBob and Patrick take a trip to the Fry Cook Museum, beautifully housed in an old stove, and SpongeBob accidentally proves himself worthy of being Neptune's royal fry cook. How so? Though many have tried and failed before him, including the buff Larry the Lobster, SpongeBob pulls the golden spatula from a mound of ancient grease (get it? Gods, ancient Greece?) while pointing someone to the menu section of the museum. It's a parody of T. H. White's Arthurian novel *The Sword in the Stone* (1938).

When Neptune suddenly appears to greet his new royal fry cook, he is in disbelief at the thought it could be someone of SpongeBob's stature and station.

"At last, someone worthy of being the royal fry cook. Who has freed the spatula from the grease?" Neptune asks the gathering crowd.

"I did, Mr. Neptune, sir. SpongeBob SquarePants," respectfully replies our protagonist, proudly holding the golden spatula.

"A fine jest, boy," says Neptune. "You are but a lowly yellow sponge. Puny. Insignificant. A commoner. Therefore, you could never be fry cook to a god. This is why it is funny. Now step aside while I seek out the true fry cook."

Only everyone in the crowd is pointing to SpongeBob.

"Ha, ha. It is even funnier the second time around," say Neptune, who begins to flex his muscles by destroying things and zapping Patrick's eyes from his face to his butt. Finally, Neptune challenges SpongeBob to a cook-off in the Atlantis Poseidome. The first to prepare one thousand patties is the winner.

Naturally, Neptune uses his magic to temporarily defeat Sponge-Bob, who loses, 1,000 patties to 1. But Neptune's magical patties are tasteless. After trying SpongeBob's singular patty, Neptune's delighted taste buds declare him the winner to the thunderous roar of the huge Poseidome crowd.

Will SpongeBob leave Bikini Bottom and his friends behind to live in a palace? No way. Instead, Neptune becomes SpongeBob's trainee at the Krusty Krab, so he can learn to cook for himself. The motto SpongeBob teaches him is a simple one: perfect patties are made with love, not magic.

A hearty lesson!

THE LEGEND OF ATLANTIS

An artist's imagined ruins of Atlantis. *Getty/StockByM*

The fictitious island nation of Atlantis stretches as far back in popular imagination as 360 BC, when it appeared in a pair of Plato's works, *Timaeus* and *Critias*. Portrayed by Plato as an antagonistic nation with an overwhelming naval power, Atlantis forced its might upon ancient Athens until Atlantis fell out of favor with the gods, who subsequently sunk the island to the bottom of the Atlantic Ocean.

In the succeeding centuries, writers and modern-day filmmakers have mostly glorified the legendary island of Atlantis as a submerged and hidden paradise. Here are just a few among the many mentions of Atlantis that you may recognize: In Jules Verne's classic sci-fi novel *20,000 Leagues under the Sea* (1869–1871), Captain Nemo visits the sunken city of Atlantis; Atlantica (Atlantis?) is the setting in Disney's *The Little Mermaid*; and DC Comics superhero Aquaman often calls Atlantis his home.

PERSPECTIVE: TOM KENNY

Q: What were your first feelings when you were introduced to the concept of SpongeBob?

TK: I felt an affinity for the character right away. It really called to me in a way that few other acting opportunities have. First seeing SpongeBob, as a drawing on loose pages, it was like being in the film *Raiders of the Lost Ark* when they first open the Ark of the Covenant and you're mesmerized by what's inside. Stephen's pages were way more embryonic than his pitch bible. It was just sketches. He said to me, "What do you think? Funny?" I don't really remember my answer to him. But what I said to myself was, "Wow! If I don't get to be the voice of this yellow guy with the square pants, tie, and striped tube socks, I'm going to be really sad and it's going to take me a long time to get over it." That was an unusual feeling for me to have because being in show business gives you thick skin, what I call "rhino skin." . . . But it was almost like meeting your potential significant other, a kind of love at first sight.

FAN FORUM

"*SpongeBob SquarePants* is special because it reminds me of my own group of real-life friends. How we're all different from each other but still closely related, just like the characters on the show. SpongeBob also means something to me because he's not afraid to stand out from everyone else. That reminds me of myself because I don't like to dress or act like other people either."—E. C.

THE SECOND HALF
OF SEASON I
(EPISODES II-20)

SELF-IMAGE

In "MuscleBob BuffPants" (season 1, episode 11), our slender-armed sponge has some doubts about his self-image. His exercise routine of lifting weights—a stuffed rabbit and teddy bear suspended from either end of a thin wooden stick—simply isn't cutting it. "This working out thing isn't working out," concludes SpongeBob. That's when a TV commercial pitchman (sorry, I mean "pitchshark") introduces SpongeBob to Anchor Arms, rubberized arm coverings that blow up like balloons to your desired muscle size.

"Hey you, wimpy, wimpy, wimpy. . . . Are you a weakling, built like a sponge? Well, now you too can have muscles with Anchor Arms. They slip on like a glove, just add air. . . . I was a wimp before Anchor Arms. Now I'm a jerk and everybody loves me," says the flexing shark.

SpongeBob takes the plunge and purchases the product, possibly using his MasterCarp credit card. Our protagonist shows off his pumped-up biceps at Mussel Beach, Hillenburg's terrific parody of California's Muscle Beach, where bodybuilding attracted its first wave of media attention in the 1930s. The crowd is in awe of SpongeBob's new physique.

"I remember when I used to look like that guy over there," says an ego-inflated SpongeBob, pointing to a scrawny fish.

When pressed about his improved workout routine, our clueless sponge does arms farts, and the muscle-headed crowd, eager to look like him, performs them too.

Sandy Cheeks is impressed and enters her faux-muscled friend into an anchor-tossing contest. It's a funfest of comical avoidance as SpongeBob does everything humanly—sorry, *spongely*—possible to avoid competing.

Only he can't. Sandy's simply too insistent.

When put to the test, SpongeBob's Anchor Arms eventually explode, leaving them flapping like a flailing inflatable tube man.

After SpongeBob makes amends for his deception, he and Sandy devise the perfect workout routine for him. Push-ups and sit-ups? No chance. Instead, they sit in front of TV while SpongeBob counts off the number of times he clicks the remote.

SAYING GOODBYE

The second half of season 1 continues to answer questions about life in this underwater society. For example, do its citizens ever die? Apparently so.

When SpongeBob and Patrick believe they've accidentally killed their neighbor in "Squidward the Unfriendly Ghost" (season 1, episode 11), the pair gets him a coffin, digs a grave, and invites mourners to his impending funeral service.

"Oh Squidward, we all came as soon as we were sure you were dead," says a gently sobbing Mr. Krabs.

There are also hooks that occasionally appear on the outskirts of town, which can haul Bikini Bottom residents to the surface, where they might be cooked, eaten, sold at a gift shop, or even worse, vacuum-packed in a can.

Citizens can also catch Suds, an equivalent to our flu. The cure? For SpongeBob, it's a trip to the hospital in "Suds" (season 1, episode 15). That's where a fish physician prescribes a sponge treatment for him—getting soaped up by a giant human hand named "Hans" and used to scrub dishes, a car, and someone's back in the shower in scenes borrowed from our surface world. (That's Tom Kenny's back, by the way.)

WORDS OR IMAGES?

In "Employee of the Month" (season 1, episode 12), SpongeBob claims to have been chosen by Mr. Krabs as employee of the month for twenty-six consecutive months. But if you carefully scrutinize the display of photos on the wall of the Krusty Krab recognizing the past winners, you'll see that SpongeBob's likeness appears in all forty-three frames—four rows of nine and a fifth row of seven (forty-three in total), with a single empty frame ending that final row.

What's up with that, writers and animators? Didn't you think we'd count?

I-M-A-G-I-N-A-T-I-O-N

H. G. Wells's novella *The Time Machine* (1985) is generally credited with popularizing the idea of time travel. Stephen Hillenburg comically employs that theme when he sends Squidward time traveling in "SpongeBob 129" (season 1, episode 14) via the Krusty Krab's walk-in refrigerator. How does that work out for Squidward? Very annoyingly. The forty-first century is full of SpongeBob and the robotlike SpongeTrons—the original and 486 clones of himself.

The prehistoric past is inhabited by primitive versions of SpongeBob and Patrick, who fear jellyfish until Squidward teaches them how to use nets for jellyfishing.

Unable to endure either the future or the past, Squidward begs to be alone. That wish is granted when he breaks into an alternative universe where his only company is the literal representation of the word "alone."

Squidward then recants all of his complaints, asking only to be returned home to his own time. Upon his return, Squidward turns to SpongeBob and Patrick, who are holding jellyfishing nets, and asks, "Who's the barnacle head who invented that game anyway?" Their answer, in true ironic-twist fashion, "You are, Squidward."

HOW OLD IS SPONGEBOB SQUAREPANTS?

What is SpongeBob's age? That's a commonly asked question, and creator Stephen Hillenburg seemingly gives the answer in a dream sequence that occurs during the premiere season's fifteenth episode, titled "Sleepy Time." SpongeBob dreams that he has his boating license, which displays his address, 124 Conch Street, and his date of birth as July 14, 1986. The episode first aired in January 2000. That would make SpongeBob approximately six months shy of his fourteenth birthday. Need to know how old SpongeBob is today? Simply do the math.

SpongeBob, whose zodiac sign is Cancer, represented by a crab, perfect for a sea creature, shares the same birthdate with former US president Gerald Ford, actress Jane Lynch, and mixed martial artist Conor McGregor.

5

PATRICK STAR

COMEDY FROM BIG PINK

SpongeBob's best friend and sidekick is Patrick Star (voiced by Bill Fagerbakke), a pink starfish who resides two doors down from our spongy protagonist at 120 Conch Street beneath a large brown rock. Wait, do rocks even have doors? It doesn't matter in this case, because despite his rather large girth, Patrick simply slides beneath his rock, which also flips opens, as if hinged, to enter and exit. It's interesting to note that Stephen Hillenburg's original sketches of Patrick's rock home contain a doorbell that rings with a "ding-dong."

The starfish, normally clad in green Hawaiian-style shorts with purple flowers similar to those dotting Bikini Bottom's skies, is incredibly loyal to his friend. Sure, there are disagreements between the pair and even extreme temper tantrums on the part of Patrick, whose emotions can overtake his fun-loving nature like a runaway tidal wave. But in the comedic end, Patrick always has SpongeBob's back, even when he unknowingly mistakes SpongeBob's back for his front. No kidding.

A starfish on the beach at sunrise. Patrick still must be napping on his rock. *Getty/valio84sl*

"Patrick acts as the gas to Sponge Boy's fire, increasing the potential for catastrophe for everyone around them, including Patrick. But whatever happens, Patrick always remains a loyal friend," noted Stephen Hillenburg in the pitch bible for the series.

THE VILLAGE IDIOT?

What about Patrick's IQ? Is he really the village idiot of Bikini Bottom? Well, it all depends on the circumstance. When called upon to fill in behind the register for Squidward, Patrick answers the phone to a customer wanting to know, "Is this the Krusty Krab?" His straightforward reply? "No. This is Patrick." That exact exchange occurs three times in quick succession with three different customers—while the clueless Patrick gets more frustrated after each call.

"I am not a crusty crab," insists Patrick.

Finally, SpongeBob intercedes and calms his friend by informing him that the Krusty Krab is the name of the restaurant.

That's standard for simple Patrick, who believes that the fishing hooks descending into the waters just outside of town are carnival rides and the bearers of free cheese samples in the episode "Hooky" (season 1, episode 20).

"I sense no danger here," proclaims Patrick, helping himself to a tasty morsel from a baited hook.

But every so often, Hillenburg beautifully counterbalances the simple Patrick with a savant—someone of average or less-than-average intelligence who possesses superior knowledge in a particular area or subject.

Here's an example of savant Patrick: "You may be an open book, SpongeBob, but I'm a bit more complicated than that. The inner machinations of my mind are an enigma," says Patrick, comparing their personalities.

I suppose you never imagined that Patrick Star would make you run for a dictionary. I'll save you the trouble: *machination* is defined as the act of scheming or plotting, and an enigma is something mysterious or puzzling.

There also have been times when Patrick has gained incredible intelligence for extended periods, usually due to some type of blow to the head. That change often creates a new dynamic and a startling disconnect between Patrick and SpongeBob.

"I find all of this laughter to be highly illogical," says an erudite Patrick in Hillenburg's homage to Mr. Spock from *Star Trek*. "Mr. SquarePants, I find your humor vulgar."

But even a streak of smarts can't keep this duo from their natural course—the perfect blend of protagonist and foil, no matter which one plays the lead.

"Are you sure you want to give up being smart and sophisticated to be my friend again?" asks SpongeBob, preparing to reverse Patrick's newfound intellect.

"Knowledge can never replace friendship. I prefer to be an idiot," states the starfish.

"Not just an idiot, Patrick. You're also my pal," affirms SpongeBob in a touching exchange.

At his most confused moments, Patrick believes that claustrophobia (a fear of closed-in places) means a fear of Santa Claus and that mirrors might actually be gateways to parallel universes.

So much for savant Patrick!

PERSPECTIVE: TOM KENNY

Q: SpongeBob and Patrick have a magical rapport. Are any of the lines ever improvised, and if so, how does that work?

TK: Because we all record together, they keep me and Bill [the voice of Patrick] in separate booths. So whenever we ad-lib or improvise lines, he and I can see each other. But with each of us being in separate booths, we can keep a specific take of mine or Bill's without the sound bleeding over between the two mics.

REAL-LIFE CLOSENESS TOO

In 2020, researchers named a newly recognized species of starfish *Astrolirus patricki*, honoring the character Patrick Star. Why? The species was found in the depths of the Pacific Ocean where our character supposedly lives. But there is another connection as well. It seems that these types of starfish are almost always attached to sponges. How's that for a case of real-life science mirroring our cartoon world?

SHINING STAR OF THE SECOND SEASON

Patrick really shines during the second season of *SpongeBob SquarePants* and stars in a pair of episodes: "Big Pink Loser" (season 2, episode 3) and "I'm with Stupid" (season 2, episode 17).

In "Big Pink Loser" the Bikini Bottom Postal Service (I wonder who they commemorate on their stamps. Dory? Nemo?) mistakenly delivers a package intended for SpongeBob to Patrick. There's a trophy inside that reads: "Outstanding Achievement in Achievement." Patrick is completely stoked, truly believing he's won his first-ever award. That is, until his best friend hesitantly points out the name on it: SpongeBob SquarePants. "That's a funny way to spell my name," ponders Patrick.

Upon recognizing his error, it doesn't take long until Patrick is overtaken with both jealousy and the inner desire to achieve something more in life than napping on a sun-warmed rock. He decides to win an award of his own.

"I want to defeat the giant monkey man and save the ninth dimension," says an excited Patrick, referencing a sci-fi saga.

"That sounds a little hard," says SpongeBob, asking his friend to consider something more realistic.

"How about we defeat the little monkey man and save the eighth dimension?" replies Patrick, scaling down his ambitions.

Ultimately, the normally unemployed Patrick decides to become more like the award-winning SpongeBob and take a job at the Krusty Krab. There's only one problem: the starfish with the ravenous appetite finds delivering krabby patties to customers' tables without devouring them to be an impossible task. Patrick even sweeps the floor using the wrong end of the broom.

The comedy turns to sympathy when a customer asks Patrick, "Hey, pal, did you just blow in from Stupid Town?"

So Patrick decides to copy every move that SpongeBob makes, including dressing exactly like him. That gives Hillenburg and the writers their cue to make the audience privy to the world's greatest and most annoying game of "copy me/stop copying me!"

Their nerves completely jangled by the mimicking movements and speech, each takes a deep breath and a step back from the activity. Hilariously, the audience discovers that SpongeBob and Patrick are

SpongeBob and Patrick always have each other's backs. *Paramount/Photofest © Paramount Pictures*

independently and simultaneously thinking to themselves *at least I'm safe inside my mind.*

SpongeBob then resorts to reverse psychology. He dresses like Patrick so that his friend will be inspired to become himself again. A neat trick.

"What's so great about being a big pink loser?" asks Patrick, still dressed as SpongeBob, in a moment of self-deprecating reflection.

Suddenly, a delivery truck pulls up to the embattled pair and drops off another package. Patrick stews over the thought that it's another trophy for SpongeBob, but when the package is opened, the award inside reads: "For Doing Absolutely Nothing Absolutely Longer Than Anyone Else—Patrick."

"Patrick, this trophy's for you!" exclaims SpongeBob as the best friends celebrate.

What's Patrick's next move? Why, to defend his newly won title and take a long snooze.

Now who do you think ordered that trophy?

BENEATH THE SURFACE

"Big Pink Loser" is Hillenburg's first episode in which the green-eyed monster of jealousy rears its ugly head between friends. It takes on a real issue while also illustrating how silly rivalry can seem in such a hollow disagreement. In the end, the feud appears to be resolved by some cheap gold-plated hardware. But in reality, it was the strong ties of friendship and the notion of putting someone else's needs ahead of your own.

MOM AND DAD?

We get a chance to meet Patrick's parents in "I'm with Stupid." Well, sort of. SpongeBob comes upon Patrick frantically cleaning his living room space (in this episode Patrick actually has a kitchen as well). A surprised SpongeBob comments, "The only thing I've ever seen you clean is your plate."

Patrick is intent on making a good impression because his parents believe he's dumber than a sack of diapers. A message from them reads: "Your mom and I are coming out tomorrow for Starfish Day. Try to remember. But don't try too hard or you'll hurt yourself like last time."

That's when Stephen Hillenburg takes the opportunity to poke fun at the very medium through which his creations are delivered. "If your parents think you're dumb, then they must not know what dumb really is," asserts SpongeBob, leading Patrick to counter, "But don't they watch television?"

SpongeBob offers to play dumber-than-dumb in order to convince Patrick's parents that their son is a genius. Patrick is enthralled by the plan but ponders aloud, "Don't geniuses live in lamps?"

Patrick's parents arrive and are incredibly condescending, insulting their son's intelligence at every turn. Then SpongeBob shows up, acting as if he hasn't a brain cell in his entire spongy body. But Patrick and his parents go completely overboard in belittling SpongeBob.

"Dumb people are always blissfully unaware of how dumb they really are," Patrick chides his well-meaning friend.

But when SpongeBob has had enough of the act, he can't convince either Patrick (part of the joke is that he's actually forgotten their plan) or his parents of his real cognitive skills. They all believe that Patrick just taught SpongeBob to speak in complete sentences.

Patrick receives a hug from his proud father, who now sees him in a new light and says, "I feel like I'm really meeting you for the first time." Turning to Patrick's mom, he continues, "Isn't that right, Janet?" She responds, "You bet, Marty."

"Janet? Marty? Who are you people?" shouts a suddenly enraged Patrick, realizing these aren't his parents at all.

A doorbell rings (again, on a doorless rock?). It's Squidward with Patrick's real parents, who'd been standing outside his stone head home all day, asking, "Where's Patrick?"

"Mom! Dad!" says Patrick, rushing into their arms.

"Wow, son," says his real father. "You actually recognized us this time."

By the way, their names are Herb and Margie Star.

I–M–A–G–I–N–A–T–I–O–N

Starting in the second season of *SpongeBob SquarePants*, the furniture and appliances in Patrick's house are made of sand instead of materials such as wood, glass, or metal. That means Patrick can shape these things anyway he wants. Need a new TV? Not a problem. Just grab a handful of sand and start sculpting. The concept of free furniture and household goods actually works out quite well for an unemployed starfish.

Next time you're at the beach with a bucket and pail, see what you can build. Perhaps a lounge chair to watch the tide roll in.

QUIZ QUESTION 5

Patrick sets his alarm clock to wake himself up every morning at 3:00 to do what?

The answer can be found after the book's conclusion.

6

SQUIDWARD Q. TENTACLES

THE ART OF SARCASM

Squidward Quincy Tentacles, voiced by Rodger Bumpass, is an incredibly enigmatic yet vital character to the social web that Stephen Hillenburg has created for us. Why is Squidward so difficult to understand? This octopus—ironically named Squid (who even wears an apron that reads "Kiss the Squid")—is one of a close trio of friends that includes SpongeBob and Patrick. Well, sort of. Squidward, the cashier at the Krusty Krab and next-door neighbor of the aforementioned pair, rarely admits his true feelings of friendship for them. He has an inherent need to feel superior and mentally above their silliness.

The bulbous-headed Squidward, who has attended BBU (Bikini Bottom University) and Music Arts Academy, is serious about the world and the arts, including music, painting, sculpting, and literature. Whereas Squidward plays the clarinet, SpongeBob plays the nose flute and Patrick uses his belly as a drum. SpongeBob and Patrick enjoy themselves with a myriad of games, pursuits, and pleasing pastimes while Squidward is waiting to be discovered as a huge talent by the Barnacle Bay Art Museum, though artistic talent is something in which he's lacking.

Giving an upbeat critique of Squidward's clarinet playing, SpongeBob readily comments, "I thought all those bad notes you played made it seem more original."

In his pitch bible, Stephen Hillenburg writes, "Squidward lives his life annoyed. The Crusty Crab annoys him. The customers annoy him. The boss annoys him. The vinyl seats annoy him. But most of all, Sponge Boy annoys him."

But part of Hillenburg's magic formula is that SpongeBob, and to a lesser extent Patrick, never catches on to Squidward's supreme annoyance with them.

"Do you know what today is?" asks SpongeBob.

"Annoy Squidward Day?" responds Squidward.

"No, silly. That's on the fifteenth," says SpongeBob, pointing to a calendar with the date already circled in red.

Hillenburg notes, "Sponge Boy, on the other hand, thinks he and Squidward are the lunch shift dream team—the stuff deep-fried legends are made of! Squidward and Sponge Boy are often thrown together in situations—company camping trips, wayward pizza deliveries, oboe/ukulele jam sessions—where inevitably Sponge Boy drives the snooty octopus crazy."

But whenever Squidward pushes his sarcastic nature too far, hurting SpongeBob's feelings, there's always a moment of revealing truth on the horizon for the cephalopod, who has six tentacles rather than eight because Hillenburg found him easier to draw that way.

When Squidward's misguided April Fools' Day prank causes SpongeBob to cry in "Fools in April" (season 1, episode 19), Squidward must reveal himself to make amends.

"Alright, I'm sorry. I'm sorry. I admit it. I'm sorry. I didn't mean to hurt you. In fact, SpongeBob, I like you. I like living next door. I like hearing your foghorn alarm in the morning and your high-pitched giggling at night. I also like Gary, Patrick, Sandy, Mr. Krabs, and all the other people I'm forced to be in contact with," confesses Squidward in a flood of truthful emotion.

Squidward can only dream of being as sleek as the real-life octopus. *Getty/TheSP4N1SH*

"Squidward, is all that true?" asks SpongeBob, peeking out from behind his pineapple's door. "Yes, SpongeBob. Yes, it's all true . . . but you have to promise not to tell anybody," begs Squidward.

That's when SpongeBob swings the door open wide and we see that half of Bikini Bottom is inside listening to Squidward's speech and in unison screams, "April Fools'!"

Recognizing that he's been had, Squidward slowly has a conniption before backing away and announcing, "You're right. April Fools'. I just fooled you all!"

However, the audience knows better and doesn't believe a word of Squidward's charade.

FOR THE SQUID OF IT

Our stuck-up, pessimistic cephalopod reads *Frown Digest*, keeps a rubber ducky in his tub, and wears two pairs of bunny slippers on his four appendages that serve as feet. Squidward is also responsible for a dance craze (not in Bikini Bottom, where it was booed, but rather in our world) called the Squid, in which his appendages pulse wildly to techno music in the episode "Culture Shock" (season 1, episode 10).

Has Squidward, who has an abnormal number of self-portraits hanging in his house, ever won an award? Yes. He was recognized for being Bikini Bottom's "Most Miserable Cashier." An accolade he truly earned all on his own. Just imagine Squidward's acceptance speech: *Please come again when I'm not on duty.*

EASTER ISLAND HEAD

Squidward lives in a type of moai (pronounced *MOH-eye*), which is a human figure carved from a single stone by the Rapa Nui people on Easter Island in eastern Polynesia, probably between 1250 and 1500. Today, Easter Island (actually part of Chile) sports nearly eleven hundred of these figures, with many of them lining the Pacific island's perimeter. The figures have complete bodies with hugely oversized heads. Squidward's Bikini Bottom home is solely the head, though, without the body. Squidward even refers to it as "my Easter Island head."

SECOND-SEASON SQUID

Hillenburg shines a much-deserved spotlight on Squidward by starring him in a pair of classic second-season episodes. In "Squid's Day Off" (season 2, episode 1), Squidward longingly looks out the window of the Krusty

Krab during a customer-less Sunday afternoon and scowls to himself, "It's a beautiful day and I'm stuck here in a prison of high cholesterol."

Then fortune strikes, literally, when Mr. Krabs injures himself chasing a dime down a drain. As he's being carted off to the hospital, Mr. Krabs puts Squidward in charge.

"Get well soon. Hurry back. You're in our thoughts," says Squidward with an obvious twinge of sarcasm.

The self-absorbed Squidward then puts SpongeBob in charge of both the grill and the cash register, giving himself the opportunity to leave the restaurant to run some "boss-like errands," which is code for taking the day off with pay. The naive SpongeBob is thrilled to be working both stations.

"I can't believe this is really happening. Today, I start living," proclaims the grateful sponge.

Once away from the restaurant, however, Squidward can't enjoy himself, worrying that SpongeBob will somehow destroy the place. Several times, he hurries back to the Krusty Krab, only to discover that everything is quiet, whereupon SpongeBob asks, "How are those errands going?"

Neither sunbathing nor relaxing in a pink bubble bath can calm Squidward's fears of an impending sponge-inspired disaster—like a five-alarm fire (under water?). He starts hallucinating, seeing SpongeBob, whom he refers to as a "yellow headache," everywhere. Ultimately, he springs from his tub naked, strategically covered by a ring of bubbles, and rushes to the Krusty Krab one more time.

But everything is peaceful in the still customer-less restaurant.

As the last of Squidward's modesty bubbles bursts, he's forced to wear SpongeBob's square pants. Then SpongeBob, in his tighty-whities, realizes that he had never flipped the sign in the Krusty Krab's window from "closed" to "open."

It's the final ironic straw in completely ruining Squidward's stolen day off.

BENEATH THE SURFACE

The characters have a conscience. They make decisions and there are consequences, often internal ones. Squidward knows that he's doing wrong in "Squid's Day Off" and his conscience won't allow him to benefit from it. We see this scenario again later in the series with Mr. Krabs, Mrs. Puff, and even Plankton, whose personality is driven by succeeding by any possible means.

MIRROR IMAGES

When SpongeBob and Patrick accidentally destroy Squidward's Easter Island head home while playing with a pair of reef blowers, Squidward becomes so angry that he vows to move away from Bikini Bottom in "Squidsville" (season 2, episode 6).

"I'm going to move so far away that I'll be able to brag about it," says the enraged octopus.

"Squidward, you're steaming. You're like a steamed vegetable, only smarter," observes SpongeBob, further irking his now-homeless neighbor.

But where will Squidward go?

Cue a commercial for a gated housing community playing on Squidward's badly battered TV set. It's an ad for Tentacle Arms, where happiness is just a suction cup away.

Hmm. . . . Sounds like a tagline aimed at a particular species of sea creature.

Squidward arrives at Tentacle Arms to find that it's surrounded by tall golden gates, with a squawk box at the doors asking, "Are you now or have you ever been a sponge?. . . How about a . . . " Anticipating the second question, Squidward interrupts and declares, "No. No starfish."

The gates open and Squidward enters a community where everyone—all octopi—is equally as snooty as he is. They even enjoy the same pursuits and are the exact shade of turquoise as he is. The homes are rows and rows of Easter Island heads. "Not a pineapple in sight," says an elated Squidward. "I'm finally among my own kind."

What follows is a strict daily routine of bike riding, shopping (for canned bread, of all things), interpretive dance class, and playing clarinet in a foursome that adheres to the sheet music note for note, without deviation. For Squidward, though, who somewhere deep inside has had the seeds of silliness sown into his soul by SpongeBob and Patrick, the routine goes from heavenly to repetitive to incredibly boring and, finally, lifeless.

Then Squidward spots a yard worker with a reef blower. Remembering the fun SpongeBob and Patrick had with one, Squidward swipes it and runs around causing havoc with the windy machine. In an uproar, seemingly half the population of Tentacle Arms chases after and corners Squidward, presenting a "well thought-out and organized list of complaints."

Meanwhile SpongeBob and Patrick have broken through the gated security system meant to keep their kind out. They're here to talk their friend into coming home. But everyone they encounter looks like Squidward, and they can't find him.

"Any one of these Squidwards could be the real Squidward," says SpongeBob.

That's when Stephen Hillenburg reaches for some incredible irony and has Squidward escape the angry throng by using the reef blower as a jetpack to fly back toward Bikini Bottom.

Sailing out of sight, Squidward is laughing, having the time of his life with the reef blower. That causes SpongeBob to look skyward and declare, "Well, we know one thing, [the real Squidward] sure isn't that guy."

I-M-A-G-I-N-A-T-I-O-N

Stephen Hillenburg sets SpongeBob apart from a host of other classic animated characters by his ability to rely on himself for entertainment. This ability absolutely shines in "The Paper" (season 1, episode 16).

Squidward tosses a used gum wrapper on the ground, and SpongeBob can't believe his friend doesn't want it.

"In the right hands this paper is a gold mine of entertainment," gushes SpongeBob. "A spectacular afternoon of underwater fun. A treasure-trove of . . . "

"Garbage!" interrupts Squidward, who allows SpongeBob to keep the paper, after pledging that he'll never ask for it back, no matter what.

That's all the setup Stephen Hillenburg and the writers need.

In quick succession, our porous protagonist uses the piece of paper as a cape to become SuperSponge and as a loincloth to assume the identity of SpongeBob JunglePants. He becomes a parachutist, a bull fighter, a pirate with an eye patch, and even a regular guy with an eye patch.

Eventually, Squidward yearns to have the paper back after witnessing SpongeBob's fun while playing with it. But SpongeBob doesn't want his friend to break his pledge.

Finally, as an enticement, Squidward trades SpongeBob everything he owns for it, including his Easter Island head home and, ultimately, the shirt off his back (leaving him naked except for the paper). He can actually have all the rest of his stuff back. It seems SpongeBob has had his eye on Squidward's shirt for a while.

Squidward tries his best to replicate SpongeBob's enthusiasm for that piece of paper. But honestly, who could equal SpongeBob's fun-for-the-sake-of-fun attitude?

Gary even toots away on Squidward's clarinet (oh, the slime of it), adding insult to a lack of octopus imagination.

QUIZ QUESTION 6

The first time the audience ever sees Squidward is in the premiere episode of season 1. In fact, he's cleaning graffiti off a pane of glass on the Krusty Krab's exterior. The drawing to be removed is a perfect likeness of Squidward's face with a word written above it. What is that word?

The answer can be found after the book's conclusion.

7

SANDY CHEEKS

DEEP IN THE HEART OF

Sandy's full name is Sandra Jennifer Cheeks, an anthropomorphic or human-acting squirrel. She is also the first core female character to appear in the series, beginning with the very first episode "Tea at the Treedome." Why has Sandy, who is voiced by Carolyn Lawrence, come to Bikini Bottom? A scientist and inventor by profession, she is there to study, research, and observe this society of sea creatures. Or, as Sandy likes to refer to them in her southern drawl, "critters."

That's right, southern drawl. Sandy is from Texas, the United States' second-largest state both by area and population. She has traveled more than six thousand miles from her native home to the middle of the Pacific Ocean to take this assignment for Treedome Enterprises Limited, which is run by a trio of erudite chimpanzees named Professor Percy, Dr. Marmalade, and Lord Reginald. Who would have seen that coming? I suppose the common links between the two species are peanuts and trees—only from the fertile mind of Stephen Hillenburg.

"Sandy is a thrill-seeking action girl. She is constantly attempting some death-defying stunt, and, having done just about everything imaginable above the ocean, she decided to attempt the ultimate challenge—live underneath it," observed Hillenburg in his initial plans for the series. "She is Bikini Bottom's only resident rodent and the apple of Sponge Boy's eye. She's the only one who can provide a good reason for him not to go into the Crusty Crab on his day off. Sandy looks at him as a sort of stunt buddy and usually calls the shots when they go out. Sponge Boy finds himself agreeing to the most ridiculous and impossible physical challenges just to be next to her."

SpongeBob has a total crush on Sandy, but the notion of them actually dating waned as the series moved forward. A squirrel and a sponge dating? Nothing unusual here for Hillenburg. Wait till you meet Mr. Krabs's whale of a daughter and ponder the relationship that brought her about.

Sandy is supersmart. She builds a rocket ship that can fly to the moon, where she's actually been before (has NASA heard about a squirrel in space?) in "Sandy's Rocket" (season 1, episode 8). "This is science!" affirms Sandy, a female role model Hillenburg presented two years before "STEM schools" (science, technology, engineering, and math) entered into our lexicon.

Of course, Sandy isn't all about work, and she loves to play. She is a dedicated bodybuilder, surfer, and rodeo rider. Her competitive streak takes center stage in "Karate Choppers" (season 1, episode 14), when she can't stop herself from competing in martial arts against SpongeBob, even under the threat of Mr. Krabs firing his fry cook for destroying the Krusty Krab with his errant karate chops. That competitiveness carries over to Sandy's intense pride in hailing from the Lone Star State. In the premiere season's "Texas" (episode 18), SpongeBob and Patrick attempt to entice a homesick Sandy, who has her bags packed and is ready to move back home, to the Krusty Krab for a surprise farewell party with all of her underwater friends. When she declines, they start to insult Texas. An infuriated Sandy begins to chase down the pair, who are strategically running toward the restaurant.

"Patrick, what am I now?" asks SpongeBob, transforming his body into the shape of Texas.

"Stupid?" inquires Patrick.

"No, I'm Texas," replies SpongeBob.

"What's the difference?" counters Patrick as a red-cheeked Sandy blows her top.

"Y'all best apologize or I'm going to be on you like ugly on an ape!" Sandy exclaims, her fur standing on edge.

After Sandy hogties Patrick rodeo style and accidentally destroys the front facade of the Krusty Krab, she sees all of the partygoers inside and a banner that reads: "Happy Texas."

"For me?" asks a choked-up Sandy.

The writers have a field day with Texas imagery being misinterpreted by her friends. There's square dancing, with Flats the Flounder holding a square box as he takes a dance step, Squidward in pain holding a barbed letter Q for a barbeque, and Pearl Krabs presenting a can of peas baked into a pie representing pecan pie. To top it off, Sponge-Bob and Patrick don huge water bottles on their heads in the form of ten-gallon cowboy hats.

Sandy can't help but fall to the seafloor laughing, realizing that she's already in the right place. "Home is where you're surrounded by other critters who care about you," says Sandy. "I've been home all along, and it took me until just now to realize it. . . . I'm a-stayin'."

Thank goodness. She was going to be impossible to replace with a milk cow or a potbellied pig.

THE TREEDOME

All animals need to breathe air to survive. But unlike the residents of Bikini Bottom, the gill-less Sandy isn't equipped to do it underwater without the aid of scientific ingenuity. So Sandy, who wears an air helmet whenever she's out and about with her friends, lives inside a huge plastic air-filled dome. The dome, which has a tall sturdy tree in the center of it, is aptly called the treedome. Squirrels often live in trees, and it's a fitting addition to this habitat. But both the tree and the grass that covers the ground beneath the dome aid in creating oxygen through a process called photosynthesis. Leaves and blades of grass pull in carbon dioxide and water to create sugar to feed themselves and as a byproduct produce oxygen. It's a terrific scientific design by Hillenburg for an airtight underwater domed space.

When visiting the treedome, Sandy's underwater friends typically wear a water helmet to help them breathe better in that environment.

Comically, Hillenburg places a giant hamster wheel inside the dome for Sandy to exercise. Be careful, though. Don't ever call Sandy a hamster by mistake, not unless you're looking for a down-home Texas-size tussle.

QUIZ QUESTION 7

Sandy Cheeks has a twin brother. He hasn't actually been seen in the series, only mentioned by Sandy. Do you know his name? Here's a hint: Stephen Hillenburg and the writers used a rhyme scheme to name him and help the audience remember.

The answer can be found after the book's conclusion.

THE HIBERNATION DILEMMA

The series featured a pair of second-season episodes in which Sandy prepared for her oncoming hibernation. In "Pre-Hibernation Week" (season 2, episode 7), Sandy vows to cram all of the adventure she can into the week prior to her winter-long hibernation. SpongeBob volunteers to be her thrill-seeking partner, but Sandy turns him into a yellow puddle of exhaustion with nonstop activities such as extreme sand surfing, mountain biking through the Bikini Bottom Industrial Park, searching for a piece of hay in a sharp needle stack (cleverly inverted by the writers), and even skydiving from the top of the tall Sea Needle, a takeoff of Seattle's iconic Space Needle structure, which stands 605 feet tall.

But before the pair can go atom smashing, SpongeBob hides himself under Patrick's rock to rescue himself from Sandy's thrill-seeking madness. Believing SpongeBob has gone missing, Sandy enlists the entire town to search for him. Hillenburg even creates a "lost" poster featuring an early image of Sponge Boy. By the time SpongeBob is eventually found, and he must tell Sandy the truth—that prehibernation week is too intense for him—she literally falls asleep on her feet.

In "Survival of the Idiots" (season 2, episode 9), SpongeBob and Patrick visit the hibernating Sandy in the treedome, where winter has arrived and the dome is filled with snow. The blithering pair accidentally awake the sleeping squirrel, who dreams they're Texan desperadoes named Dirty Dan and Pinhead Larry, and she gives them a personal tour of "Hurtsville."

Both hibernation-themed episodes are classics, but in actuality, Stephen Hillenburg is throwing the audience a massive curve here. Why? Well, tree squirrels don't hibernate. Sure, they change their daily activities during winter, slowing down to conserve energy while food is in shorter supply, but they don't actually sleep through the season.

One more blip. SpongeBob and Patrick spend nearly the entire episode, from winter until spring, in the treedome. But they do it without the assistance of water helmets for breathing. Was this a forgetful mistake on the part of Hillenburg and the writers? Or was it purposely done to aid in the characters' illustrations, actions, and speech during such an extended period in that environment?

What do you think?

I-M-A-G-I-N-A-T-I-O-N

In a rare moment of insecurity, Sandy worries that her three chimp bosses, who are visiting from the surface world, will fire her because her inventions (including an automated nutcracker and a helmet that enables you to talk to nuts—what else would a squirrel invent?) aren't up to par and fire her. That's when SpongeBob and Patrick, posing as Mr. Doctor-Professor Patrick, attempt to help Sandy by inventing an automatic back-scratching, hair-combing, nose-picking ukulele tuner.

Together, let's all channel our inner Squidward and say, "Yeah, that's a better idea."

The pair test their goofy invention on Sandy's bosses.

"That horrible screaming means that it's working," Mr. Doctor-Professor Patrick assures them.

When the invention completely falls apart, Sandy's automated nut-cracker suddenly snaps to life and peels a banana for the chimps, who go wild with excitement and praise for Sandy.

What do they want to see invented via her brilliant imagination next? An automatic poop-throwing machine. Visit the monkey house in any zoo, and you'll understand exactly why.

MULTI-MOVIE PARODY

Sandy Cheeks playing the part of Bruce Lee? Well, Bruce Lee didn't do karate like Sandy. He studied kung fu and then created his own martial art called *jeet kune do*, which translates to "the way of the intercepting fist" in Cantonese. But in "Karate Island" (season 4, episode 11), Stephen Hillenburg and the writers/illustrators dress Sandy in a yellow jumpsuit with a black stripe exactly like Bruce Lee wore in the classic martial arts film *Game of Death* (1978).

SpongeBob receives a videotape in the mail inviting him to Karate Island to participate in a tournament where the winner will be named king of karate. Yes, I know. That's basically the plot of a different Bruce Lee movie titled *Enter the Dragon* (1973). But the writers actually shuffle movies once more when actor Pat Morita, who played Mr. Miyagi in *The Karate Kid* (1984), voices the character of Master Udon on Karate Island. Sandy, who has accompanied SpongeBob to the island competition, immediately realizes that something is afoul and defeats an array of different opponents (as Lee does in *Game of Death*) to rescue her friend.

Sandy is correct. The competition is a scheme by the shifty Master Udon, whose real interest is selling SpongeBob a vacation time-share on the island.

Moments after we see SpongeBob and Sandy escape Master Udon's clutches, Squidward is ushered onto the island via boat.

"I'm here!" announces Squidward. "The king of clarinets has arrived!"

That's the real estate game for you.

FAN FORUM

"*SpongeBob* was my whole childhood, and it was always playing on the TV. It was also great for me and my brother because it was something we could bond over. We really didn't have much in common, except for *SpongeBob SquarePants*. Understanding that it was something we could both enjoy was very special to me. The show always made us laugh, even when we were having a bad day. It was always an escape and something we could watch just to get away from our surroundings for a while."—O. S.

TURKEY DAY PARADE

How would you like to look out the window of a Manhattan high-rise apartment building and suddenly come face-to-face with an immense replica of our yellow porous protagonist? Well, if you're in New York City in late November, it could happen.

The Macy's Thanksgiving Day Parade, which boasts a nearly one-hundred-year history of amazing floats

The new SpongeBob and Gary (riding on his back) balloon sails down the streets of Manhattan in the 2022 Macy's Thanksgiving Day Parade. *Photo by Eugene Gologursky/Getty Images for Macy's, Inc.*

and gigantic helium balloons, takes place on the streets of Manhattan and is broadcast around the country. The parade's current fan favorite and heaviest balloon ever, weighing a staggering 896 pounds, is SpongeBob SquarePants. The resident of Bikini Bottom is raising his arms in victory with Gary, his pet snail, riding upon his back. Its excessive weight means that in bad weather, such as high winter winds, SpongeBob is among the first balloons grounded for safety reasons. So keep your fingers crossed for a clam . . . I mean, a calm day. The current balloon, the third incarnation of SpongeBob in the parade, made its debut in 2019 and was designed by Laura Duphiney and Erik Payne. It requires 18,000 cubic feet of helium to fill the balloon and takes ninety handlers on the ground to keep it flying straight.

"Oh, yeah, I was definitely a fan of *SpongeBob* growing up as a kid, and I occasionally still watch it on TV," said Laura Duphiney, an artist and design specialist. "There's a whole process to designing a balloon for the parade. First, I had to meet with representatives of Nickelodeon, who needed to approve the sketches and concept for the character's pose. Then there are schematics and figuring out where the mast will sit. The mast is the compartment that will contain the most helium. Next, a 3D model needs to be made to see what kind of problems might occur during flight. Finally, the balloon gets assembled with all the seams being glued, never sewn, because the helium might escape."

Laura Duphiney has held nearly every job along the two-and-a-half-mile parade route, working an exhausting twenty-four consecutive hours during the holiday to accomplish the task. "It's just always a special feeling to watch a balloon you've designed fly, especially Sponge-Bob," said Duphiney, who has designed a total of fifteen balloons for the parade over the years, including another two-character balloon in Snoopy and Woodstock.[1]

SpongeBob is the parade's only square balloon, and the shape makes it much harder to keep in top condition. The original SpongeBob balloon (designed by Jerry Ospa) joined the parade in 2004, just five years after the character's series began. That was the tallest SpongeBob balloon, measuring sixty-two feet. The two subsequent balloons were less than forty-five feet tall. The one Duphiney designed flew from 2004 to 2006 and 2008 to 2012 before its condition deteriorated and the balloon needed to be replaced.

The second balloon (designed by Harry Moore), which flew from 2013 to 2018, shows SpongeBob sporting a Santa hat because he was Macy's Parade ambassador during that period and had the honor of being the final balloon in the parade.

Other Nickelodeon characters that have had balloons in the parade include Papa Smurf, Chase from *PAW Patrol*, Rugrats, Blue from *Blue's Clues*, and Jimmy Neutron.

PERSPECTIVE: TOM KENNY

Q: How badly did you want the role of SpongeBob?

TK: I knew I was the perfect guy to be SpongeBob. Stephen didn't audition anyone else and told me, "You've got the gig." That was gutsy of him because he didn't have that kind of power at that point. He had the logic of *Star Trek*'s Mr. Spock and the passion of Captain Kirk and Dr. Bones McCoy. The network wanted to read lots of other people and had even discussed getting a Hollywood star to voice the character.

Not only did I see myself as SpongeBob, Stephen had envisioned me in the role even before showing me the character. He said, "There's lots of you in the character, Tom. He's high energy, hyperactive, works super hard, and sometimes people don't understand the passions that drive him." I was just fortunate enough to be in Stephen's orbit for him to see those things, with us both having worked on *Rocko's Modern Life*.

SHELL-PHONE RINGING

Believe it or not, there are currently ninety-three people in the United States who have their phone numbers listed under the name SpongeBob SquarePants. They are scattered across the country in locales such as Columbus, Ohio; Clifton, Colorado; St. James, Missouri; Boise, Idaho; Derby, Kansas; and Kissimmee, Florida. The state of New York has the most SpongeBob SquarePants listings with eight, California and Florida each have seven, and Pennsylvania has six.

If for some reason you decide to look one of these numbers up in order to give SpongeBob a call, please don't do it without a parent on the line with you. And be sure you have a relevant SpongeBob question to ask, such as, "What's the area code for Bikini Bottom?" Also, I can assure you that none of these phone numbers belong to the character's voice, Tom Kenny. I promise.

YOU SHOULD HAVE KNOWN BETTER

If you saw the online advertisements for a show titled *A Day with SpongeBob SquarePants: The Movie* and believed it was real, you should have known better. The supposed premise is that SpongeBob's agent tells him that his career is slipping. To garner publicity, a contest is arranged for a lucky real-life fan to spend the day with SpongeBob in Hollywood. The winner is named Seth and his day with our porous protagonist becomes a roller-coaster ride of comical ups and downs. That's how the imagined script was planned for this "mockumentary" by a company called Reagal Films. There was even a movie poster with a trio of fake reviews and young Seth's photo attached, as well as talk of a crowd-funding campaign to finance the film. But, alas, the imagined big-screen parody was nothing more than a tease for loyal fans.

8

MR. KRABS AND PEARL

MORE THAN A FAST BUCK

"Hello, I'm Mr. Krabs, and I like money," says Eugene Harold Krabs, the creator of the krabby patty and owner of Bikini Bottom's premier fast-food restaurant, the Krusty Krab. If the character of Mr. Krabs, voiced by actor Clancy Brown, were so one dimensional, both the audience and SpongeBob himself would have tired of the penny-pinching proprietor rather quickly. But Stephen Hillenburg and the writers were too smart to allow that to ever occur.

Mr. Krabs is also a dedicated single parent, one who wants only the best for his trendy teenage daughter Pearl. Oh, and did I happen to mention that unlike her father, who is a red crab, Pearl is a sperm whale? There is even a photo that adorns the wall of Mr. Krabs's office of him teaching Pearl to "breach." That's when a whale breaks through the surface of the water and partly into the air. Researchers believe these aquatic mammals do this in order to communicate messages, from mating calls to changes in swimming direction to warnings about predators.

A whale breaching the surface of the water. Your turn next, Pearl! *Getty/PaulWolf*

"There she blows" is a phrase Mr. Krabs says in recognition of his daughter. It was coined (Mr. Krabs would like that) by the lookouts on whaling ships to alert the crew of a whale surfacing and spouting water from its blowhole. In his classic novel *Moby-Dick* (1851), author Herman Melville writes, "There she blows! A hump like a snow-hill. It's Moby-Dick."

By Hillenburg's own design, the audience never sees or hears about Pearl's biological mother. But interestingly enough, whenever Eugene Krabs is surprised by a situation, he often uses the expression "Mother of Pearl!" as a substitute for a non-G-rated phrase. This expression was popularized by the comedy team of Cheech and Chong in the 1970s, something the writing staff of *SpongeBob SquarePants* would have known.

But probably even more important in giving the character of Mr. Krabs depth (that's an undersea pun!) is the fact that, despite his repeated attempts to manipulate SpongeBob, usually over his paycheck, he serves as a father figure, giving our porous protagonist advice.

"Beware the hooks. . . . The hooks. They dangle down and draw you close with their shapes and beguiling colors. Then just when you think you've found the land of milk and honey, they grab you by the britches and haul you way up high . . . until you're hauled up to the surface, blubbing and gasping for breath," warns Mr. Krabs, schooling SpongeBob about the dark human art of fishing.

He is also the inventor of the restaurant's signature dish.

"Look at it. . . . Mr. Krabs's gift to all of Bikini Bottom, the krabby patty," says SpongeBob, completely in awe of his boss.

Is there any cannibalism going on here? Are krabby patties *made* of crab, or do they just bear the name of their creator, Eugene H. Krabs?

After nibbling a patty, Mr. Krabs says to himself, "So that's what I taste like." The conversation ends there, with Hillenburg and the writers giving us plenty of pause to think.

Mr. Krabs has a keen olfactory sense. Not only can he smell money, but he can also sniff out laziness in his employees, especially Squidward.

Both Mr. Krabs and Pearl live in a hollowed-out anchor, and depending on which episode you rely upon for their address, they reside at either 3451 Anchor Way ("Sleepy Time," season 1, episode 15) or 2219 Anchor Street ("Mall Girl Pearl," season 9, episode 19) per Mr. Krabs's driver's license.

QUIZ QUESTION 8

This is a two-part quiz. You can congratulate yourself if you get either question correct. But if you ace both parts, then the next round of krabby patties is on the house for you and your friends. Just don't tell Mr. Krabs. The episode "The Slumber Party" (season 6, episode 9) provides us with extended time in the anchor home during Pearl's teen slumber party. (1) What drink does Mr. Krabs keep stored in scores of barrels in his cellar? (2) Which horror movie do Pearl and her girlfriends watch on TV that night, making them extremely nervous?

The answer can be found after the book's conclusion.

PLOT-DRIVING KRABS

There are many sides to Mr. Krabs's personality, all of which are expertly used by Stephen Hillenburg and the writing staff to drive the plotlines of key episodes. Among these is the exploitive side of Mr. Krabs: the boss giving orders, not requests, both on the clock at the Krusty Krab and off.

In the third season's "Wet Painters" (episode 10), the boss has SpongeBob and Patrick paint the living room walls of his home without pay, using what is supposedly permanent paint.

"I have a *super, special, secret* assignment," says Krabs, as the eyes of the two naïfs grow wider with each successive adjective. Mr. Krabs is such a good salesman that they don't even experience a letdown after discovering the assignment is just painting. Of course, he's also a bit of a bully. If they spill any pigment on his many valued knickknacks mounted on the walls, which they must cautiously paint around, he threatens to mount their "butts" on his wall like trophies. *Just for spilling paint?*

Comically, the nervous pair spill just a single drop, but it's on Mr. Krabs's most prized possession—the first dollar that he ever earned.

What's perfectly pictured upon that dollar? No, not George Washington's deep-sea equivalent, George Herring-ton. Rather, it's a clam, which is slang for money, like the words "bread," "Benjamins," "cheddar," "dough," "cabbage," "bacon," and "Gouda," a type of cheese.

After stressing themselves to the max and making the damage even worse by trying to clean the bill, Mr. Krabs returns home and lets SpongeBob and Patrick in on a secret. This "permanent" paint can be removed with saliva, and he licks the bill clean in front of them. But the Fates rightly dictate that Mr. Krabs will not benefit from his callous behavior. He begins to laugh so hard at his own joke that he spatters the walls with saliva, and the beautiful, free paint job dissolves.

"I really got to learn to say it, not spray it," mourns a self-defeated Mr. Krabs.

In "Krusty Towers" (season 4, episode 9), Mr. Krabs travels out of town for a fast-food convention and is charged $25 for a room-service hamburger. That gives him the idea to turn the Krusty Krab into a high-rise hotel called the Krusty Towers, thereby forcing customers who want a krabby patty to rent a room and order room service.

"If they can charge that much for a lousy burger, then imagine what I can charge for a lousy krabby patty. And thus, the Krusty Towers was born," says Mr. Krabs, who dons a spiffy tux for the occasion—and for the inflated prices.

Patrick arrives at the newly opened enterprise and orders one krabby patty and one room, with cheese. "And can I get cheese on the krabby patty, too?" inquires the clueless starfish.

The hotel's motto reads: "We shall never deny a guest even the most ridiculous request."

That statement sets the stage for some outrageous comedy.

Mr. Krabs uses the motto to make bellhop Squidward comply with all of Patrick's comical whims. To get even with his boss, Squidward quits and then checks into the hotel as a guest, leaving Mr. Krabs on the hook to serve *him*. He orders a krabby patty made with some stomach-wrenching fixings. When it arrives, Squidward requests that Mr. Krabs eat it. Just as Krabs is about to refuse, SpongeBob whispers to his boss, "That's not really a krabby patty with cheese, nose hair, and toenail clippings." So Mr. Krabs swallows it whole. He looks like he's about to vomit when SpongeBob adds, "Sorry, Mr. Krabs, we were all out of cheese."

But that's just the first part of the penance the Fates and writers have in store for the greedy, price-gouging Mr. Krabs before he can be redeemed in the audience's eyes.

Squidward requests a penthouse swimming pool, and when Patrick does a cannonball dive into it, the weight of the water (wait, isn't the entire hotel under water?) brings the tall hotel crashing down, floor by floor.

With everyone lying bandaged in hospital beds, an attendant appears and hands Mr. Krabs the huge hospital bill. *Now* the scales are even.

Mr. Krabs's final thoughts on the situation?

"Forget hotels, this hospital racquet is where the money is," says Mr. Krabs before turning to the recuperating SpongeBob, Patrick, and Squidward. "Pack your bags, boys. You're going to medical school!"

I guess some crabs never learn, much to the comedic pleasure of the audience.

OLD MAN KRABS?

Mr. Krabs is substantially older than SpongeBob, Patrick, and Squidward. In fact, according to his driver's license, he was born in 1942 (you do the math to calculate his age), when Word War II was raging amid the islands of the Pacific Ocean where he undoubtedly hatched. But does Mr. Krabs ever *feel* old? He does in an episode perfectly titled "Mid-Life Crustacean" (season 3, episode 15). And for science-minded viewers: crabs, which normally live between twenty to thirty years, are classified as decapod crustaceans.

In a concerted effort to feel younger, Mr. Krabs learns some teen slang from his daughter Pearl. It seems the word "cool" has been replaced by "coral." Until she hears her dad say it. Then she quickly calls a friend to scrap that expression.

Mr. Krabs also hangs out one Saturday night with SpongeBob and Patrick. He thinks "The Wash" is a hip new club, but the uncool duo take him to a laundromat where they like to watch colorful clothes spin inside the machines.

The trio eventually embarks on a moonlit quest to purloin a pair of female underwear from a bureau drawer. (Kids: Don't attempt this at home. It's a stupid macho thing.) Krabs unwittingly breaks into his own mom's house and steals a pair of her "bloomers." He's embarrassed beyond belief when they're caught. Mr. Krabs's enraged mom punishes her son by sending him to his childhood bedroom. While lying in his former racecar-style bed, Mr. Krabs ironically admits, "I certainly feel younger."

PEARL'S PLACE

Though SpongeBob is a theoretical teenager when the series begins (just shy of his fourteenth birthday), it's Pearl Krabs who plays that adolescent role to perfection, bringing the teen factor to a number of plotlines.

When Pearl, voiced by Lori Alan, needs a date for the junior prom, Mr. Krabs assigns employee SpongeBob the job of escorting her to the dance in "The Chaperone" (season 1, episode 12) so that she doesn't fall out of favor with the "in crowd" and diminish her social standing. Naturally, being seen with the uncool SpongeBob in a social setting is a challenge in itself for Pearl.

SpongeBob arrives at the anchor house on stilts, because Pearl is so much taller than he is, and with what appears to be a literal mop (without the handle) of black hair.

"At least no one will recognize you. Now listen, SpongeBob, I just want to get through this dance with my social status intact. I want to go to the prom and get my picture taken. I want to dance. Drink punch with my friends. . . . And don't do that other thing you're always doing," dictates Pearl while SpongeBob dutifully takes notes.

The audience never finds out what that "other thing" SpongeBob does in public that Pearl doesn't want to see that night. But we can certainly imagine what it is.

Despite some hilarious faux pas on the part of SpongeBob at the dance, including falling into the punch bowl and soaking it up with his porousness, Pearl eventually admits that she is having a good time, and SpongeBob wows the crowd with his new dance sensation, the Sponge.

It's a lesson in fun triumphing over worrying about what others think.

In "Barnacle Face" (season 8, episode 7), Pearl has an outbreak of barnacles and can't face her friends because of her blemished complexion. SpongeBob comically tries to remove them with his spatula, a shovel, and even a jackhammer because Mr. Krabs is too cheap to send Pearl to a dermatologist. In the end, that decision really costs Mr. Krabs, when SpongeBob and Pearl come up with a plan to decorate her blemishes with the Krabs family jewels. A diamonded-studded barnacle pimple anyone?

SPONGEBOB VERSUS PEARL

While SpongeBob works at the Krusty Krab and lives on his own, Pearl plays the semi-rebellious teen at home, challenging the rules of adult supervision. She can turn on the waterworks with a literal flood of tears, drowning out any opposing point of view. Her bedroom walls are filled with posters of musicians, models, and media stars, and she reads teen magazines like *Coral Cuties*. Pearl has friends with braces on their teeth and one named Nocturna, who dresses in a Gothlike fashion. Perhaps the biggest teen association for SpongeBob is that he is still in search of his boating license. Importantly, Pearl also adds another female perspective and voice to the cast.

TEEN COOL/JOB AT THE MALL

Trying to attract hip teen customers, Mr. Krabs brings his daughter Pearl aboard the Krusty Krab crew during her summer vacation from school in "Bossy Boots" (season 2, episode 2). She has some immediate changes in mind. Pearl renames the restaurant the Kuddly Krab, redecorates to reflect a teen vibe, and designs new pink and purple sea-flower-patterned uniforms for her father, SpongeBob, and Squidward. But the biggest change of all is that krabby patties are off the menu and salads are in. "Sal-ads?" questions SpongeBob, who experiences major anxiety when the grill and his spatula are removed from the kitchen. However, it's not a job that enthralls Pearl, who only accepted the position to please her pop, a common teen dilemma. So Pearl and SpongeBob devise a plot to get her fired, before Pearl speeds off to the Bikini Bottom Mall, the place she really wants to be, with her friends.

Seven seasons later, in "Mall Girl Pearl" (season 9, episode 19), Pearl is ready for her first real job without any nepotism involved. What's the push to suddenly work?

"I'll be an independent working woman, blazing my own trail and standing on my own two fins," says Pearl to the delight of his father, who's tired of spending his own money on what he deems to be nonsensical items such as clothes and school supplies.

But Pearl's speech doesn't really hold water. She wants a job at the mall because all of her friends are working there, and she has no one to hang out with.

At the mall, none of the "cool stores" are willing to hire Pearl because of her girth. As a whale, she literally can't fit into some of the kiosks.

Pearl eventually gets hired at Grandma's Apron, a totally uncool establishment selling perfume that smells like grandmas (for example, pills and bedpans). The character of Grandma Beatrice, the store's proprietor, is voiced by the incomparable Betty White, a pioneer of early television who continued to act until nearly a centenarian (the age of one hundred—a century old). But when Pearl's friends rudely dismiss both Beatrice and her store, they get a taste of senior power when Beatrice uses her ninja-like knitting skills to entrap them in a sweater she's knitting. After a solid hour of stories by Beatrice about the good old days, Pearl's misguided friends are ready to revise their concept of "cool."

BENEATH THE SURFACE

The episode "Mall Girl Pearl" is a powerful statement by Stephen Hillenburg and the writers concerning "cool" kids and body-shaming, as none of the cliquey store will hire Pearl. It models the idea that we really don't live in a one-size-fits-all society and that coolness can be observed in many different forms—from Goth to grandmas.

GIRL POWER

Not enough female perspectives in *SpongeBob SquarePants*? Lots of fans might agree. But in the twelfth season's "A Cabin in the Kelp" (episode 21), which is currently the first episode alphabetically in the series canon, all of the characters are female except for SpongeBob, of course.

The Gal Pals, consisting of Sandy Cheeks, Mrs. Puff, and the electronic Karen (Plankton's computer wife), set out on a camping trip into the woods, ready to adopt a new member into their circle, newbie Pearl Krabs.

During the drive into the woods, the crew has a sing-along, performing "Gal Pal Song." The lyrics include the line, "We demand equal pay." It's a pointed reference to the long struggle by women to overcome the societal practice of being paid less than men for doing the exact same job. The empowering song ends with a warning, "Cross us and you'll be chum."

Pearl believes her initiation into the group will entail an effort to scare her with a frightening ghost story told around the campfire. So she arranges for a disguised SpongeBob to sneak into their camp in an effort to scare the others first. In the end, there are more laughs than frights. But the ending is noteworthy because the characters, while running full speed toward the audience, crash into our TV screen. It's one of the few times in the series that Stephen Hillenburg and the writers take down the fourth wall between the characters and the viewers.

The episode's name owes a debt to the sci-fi/horror comedy film *The Cabin in the Woods* (2011), in which a group of college students are systematically scared by an assortment of remote-controlled monsters.

WHAT'S THE FOURTH WALL?

A performance convention, the "fourth wall" represents the imaginary or invisible wall separating the audience from the characters. For reference, most indoor scenes contain three walls, with the audience viewing the characters and their actions through an open space that normally would be occupied by a fourth wall, if there were no audience. Whenever the characters acknowledge that there is an audience watching them or perhaps even step through that open space into the viewers' reality, that is called "breaking the fourth wall."

Shakespeare uses this technique in many of his plays to create comic relief. In productions of *Peter Pan*, Peter asks the audience to applaud for Tinkerbell to revitalize her magic. At the end of the 1986 comedy *Ferris Bueller's Day Off*, director John Hughes has actor Matthew Broderick, who plays Ferris, look directly into the camera and famously instruct the audience that it's time to go home.

TOP FIVE EPISODE COUNTDOWN: NUMBER FIVE

Our countdown of the top five *SpongeBob SquarePants* episodes begins with "Krusty Krab Training Video" (season 3, episode 10). It is Stephen Hillenburg's nostalgic tribute to the company training videos of the 1970s and 1980s, such as those of McDonald's, Burger King, Wendy's, and Jack in the Box.

The episode begins with dynamic, rhythmic, pumping music, as if viewers are about to take off on the adventure of a lifetime. A series of quick cutaway shots follows, including restaurant tables, a fully stacked burger, fries, an employee hat, patties on the grill, *and the toilets.* That's right, the toilets. Well, *someone* has to clean them, and I don't think it's going to be Mr. Krabs. Hey, it will most likely be you, the new employee.

The narrator says, "If you are watching this video, then let me be the first to say 'Congratulations.' You've recently been hired by the Krusty Krab restaurant and this your first official day of training."

SpongeBob appears, playing the role of a trainee. His greatest desire? He wants to head straight to the grill and start making krabby patties. But the narrator assures the enthusiastic newbie that he has a lot to learn before that can happen.

There's background history about the restaurant and Mr. Krabs, who is seen as a youngster cheating vending machines with a quarter on a string. Yes, Mr. Krabs was even devious with regard to money even as a child. We're informed that Eugene H. Krabs fought in "the war." Most likely, the Pacific Theater of World War II, since his age fits that time period. Exactly how did the restaurant begin? Eugene Krabs took over a bankrupt retirement home called the "Rusty Krab" and added a *K* in front of its name, transforming it into a fast-food operation.

Is there a cameo by the chain's founder giving instruction? Yes. Mr. Krabs himself appears, bragging about the restaurant's modern technology, calling a spatula "an advanced patty control mechanism" and ice cubes "high-quality beverage temperature devices." Then there's a warning about becoming an employee without passion for the job, which the narrator terms a "Squidward."

SpongeBob is still anxious to get to the grill. But first he must understand the restaurant's motto: POOP. Don't stress, it's an acronym for "People Order Our Patties." What's a customer likely to order here? A sofa? An expensive haircut? No. A patty. "POOP never lets us down!" proclaims the narrator.

After scrubbing his hands clean, as per the company's personal hygiene policy (apparently even a sponge needs to wash up), SpongeBob is finally ready to make a patty. But first, he must prepare the ingredients. In a file drawer, we see a list of ingredients such as buns, lettuce, tomatoes, onions, patties, pickles, ketchup, mustard, and mayo. There's also a listing for miscellaneous items. Could those be the necessary ingredients to create krabby patties?

We then meet Patrick, playing the part of a customer. But he's completely befuddled by the narrator's voice-over, believing that the ceiling has come to life and is speaking to him. There are also warnings about those who would steal the secret formula—also known as Plankton, who operates the rival Chum Bucket restaurant across the street.

"It's time for the moment you've been waiting for," says the narrator, building his own extended orchestral accompaniment via his voice until he's out of breath. "Preparing the krabby patty."

SpongeBob genuflects at the very thought of "learning the sacred and dark secrets of how to prepare . . . the sumptuous, lip-moistening, spine-tingling, heart-stopping"—is this a high-cholesterol pun?— "pleasure center that is a krabby patty. Are you ready?"

Our trainee sponge is so excited that he can't even get his own catchphrase, "I'm ready," out of his mouth.

"Okay, the secret formula is"—then the narrator's voice quiets and the screen goes dark. Apparently, the training video breaks down at the most inopportune moment for both SpongeBob and the audience.

But it was immense fun getting there!

WHY IT GETS HIGH MARKS

"Krusty Krab Training Video" has always been one of my favorite episodes. It's like a behind-the-scenes glimpse into the Krusty Krab and what it might take to actually work there. Sign me up! The writers blend comedy and the business of fast food together so well. The narrator, voiced by Steve Kehela, is spot-on in tone (casually serious) for the era that Hillenburg is spoofing. It's a near-perfect retro tongue-in-cheek look back in time as the projector eats the final frames of the film.

9

EVOLUTION OF A SPONGE

FAMILY TREE

Throughout the *SpongeBob SquarePants* series, Stephen Hillenburg and the writers have been uniquely committed to zany and fascinating character backstories. After all, understanding a character's roots enhances our connection with them in the present and even in the future. And I mean way in the future: we've already witnessed a time-traveling Squidward encounter hundreds of robot SpongeTrons in the forty-first century. Hence, the audience has been introduced to multiple characters inhabiting branches of the SquarePants family tree. The first two such characters: Primitive SpongeBob, whom present-day Squidward meets in "SpongeBob 129" (season 1, episode 14), and SpongeGar from the third season's "Ugh" (episode 14).

Except for a small loincloth covering his privates, Primitive Sponge-Bob is naked. Maybe that's where the modern-day equivalent gets his penchant for taking his clothes off. The primordial sponge, who hangs out with a starfish-like ancestor of Patrick, sports sharp fangs and has not yet mastered any form of language other than screams, grunts, and groans. The pair apparently live in the open without shelter (even though there are plenty of rocks for primitive Patrick). They hear music for the first time when Squidward plays his clarinet. Is it true that music hath charms to soothe the savage breast? Apparently not, as they attempt to pound Squidward into the ground for his performance. Or maybe it was just his poor playing that set them off.

Hillenburg and the writers inch the timeline forward in "Ugh," hosted by Patchy the Pirate (Tom Kenny), who informs us that the episode is set one million years ago BC, or before comedy. He explains that it was a period when man struggled for survival, and dinosaurs ruled the earth. Let's remember that Tom/Patchy is a comedian and not a historian. In fact, people showed up more than sixty million years after the dinosaurs became extinct. But there were small shrew-sized mammals that shared the earth with dinosaurs. Maybe they were similar to the characters in "Ugh," which isn't set underwater in Bikini Bottom, but rather above sea level in prehistoric Encino, California. For you entertainment-history buffs, make note that there is a 1992 comedy film titled *Encino Man* (1992). In that flick, a caveman is found frozen in the earth by some Encino teens who thaw him out and introduce him to modern teen society.

Unlike primitive SpongeBob, SpongeGar lives in a prehistoric version of a pineapple, with drawings on the inside walls that record early attempts at jellyfishing. He also has developed language skills, naming individuals like Patar (prehistoric Patrick), Squog (prehistoric Squidward), and Gary, a gigantic snail-like creature and perhaps the world's first house pet.

What's the key link to primitive times and today in this episode? Well, SpongeGar and Patar discover fire when a bolt of lightning strikes a log. Almost immediately, our sponge-like character gets the idea of using fire to cook his food. Could it be that modern-day SpongeBob is actually genetically predisposed to become a fry cook? Is it programmed in his DNA to operate a grill and make krabby patties? It's certainly worth a thought.

The episode contains a pair of terrific twists, reflecting the ironic sensibilities of the series. A tiny prehistoric crab shows up, moving toward the fire and shouting, "Mine!" in a Mr. Krabs–inspired voice. Might the first fast-food digs be on the horizon? Nope. Patar cooks the crab and eats him. Eventually, the fire goes out, but Squog, who had been trying to steal the fire for himself, gets struck by the next lightning bolt and is burned to a crisp. Both SpongeGar and Patar stand over his still-smoldering body and conduct history's first recorded marshmallow roast.

The next link in the DNA chain is SpongeBob's great-great-great-grandfather SpongeBuck SquarePants, who in "Pest of the West" (season 5, episode 17) arrives in the undersea western town of Dead Eye Gulch, named for the villainous Dead Eye, a minuscule, single-eyed forefather of Bikini Bottom's own Plankton. The naive and well-mannered Sponge-Buck unwittingly becomes sheriff and is forced into a duel with Dead Eye, whom he accidentally steps on (*squish*), thus rescuing the town from Dead Eye's grip. In the present day, Sandy finds SpongeBuck's story in the library and reads it to SpongeBob. Buoyed by the heroic tale, SpongeBob

A real-life sponge on a coral reef. Perhaps a cousin of SpongeBob? *Getty/mychadre77*

cleans an old, unrecognizable statue outside of the library that is covered in jellyfish poop (better than bird poop?) with spongelike proficiency to discover that it's actually a statue of SpongeBuck. "Maybe someday people will know my name," says SpongeBob, in awe of his ancestor's fame. "Keep dreaming, SpongeBob," retorts Sandy. "Keep dreaming."

Further along the chain, we've briefly seen SpongeBob's paternal grandfather, Grandpa SquarePants, inside "thought bubbles" imagined by his grandson. Then there's his wife, aptly named Grandma SquarePants, who is a round sea sponge and not square. They're parents to SpongeBob's father, Harold SquarePants, who met and wed Margaret BubbleBottom. That pairing produced our main protagonist, who is square although both of his parents are round. I guess the square-shaped gene skipped a generation. Not surprising. Mother Nature can be a mad scientist, especially in Stephen Hillenburg's cartoon universe.

CHILD, ADULT, OR BOTH?

SpongeBob navigates the world with a pair of competing mindsets—one as a child and one as an adult. Hillenburg and the writing staff make sure that neither way of thinking ever completely dominates the other, providing the audience with plenty of laughs and food for thought. This is never more evident than in the episode "Grandma's Kisses" (season 2, episode 6), in which SpongeBob makes the daunting decision to act more like a grownup sponge.

After an afternoon of visiting with Grandma—eating freshly baked cookies, enjoying story time, and trying on sweaters created with love in every stitch—SpongeBob is dropped off at the Krusty Krab to start his afternoon shift. Just outside the restaurant, Grandma SquarePants plants a big kiss on his forehead, leaving behind a bright red lipstick imprint. The customers inside razz SpongeBob about it to no end, calling him a "Grandma's boy," until SpongeBob bolts from the restaurant in tears.

Later, Patrick offers SpongeBob advice (you know this isn't going to work out well): "You're the most adult person I know. . . . You just can't act like a baby around her. . . . You're a man now, SpongeBob, and it's time you started acting like one," says Patrick. "Allow me to demonstrate. First, puff out your chest. Now say, 'Tax exemption.' Now you must acquire a taste for free-form jazz. . . . Okay, SpongeBob, you're ready."

Interestingly, Patrick refers to SpongeBob as a person. Mr. Krabs also describes the residents of Bikini Bottom as people. This happens over and over throughout the series and probably for the best. Why? For the audience, the association helps us to see ourselves in the characters.

Later in the episode, SpongeBob and Patrick visit Grandma's house wearing fake sideburns to show that they're grownups. While Sponge-Bob abstains from all of Grandma's loving acts, Patrick immediately assumes supreme child mode, reveling in cookies, being read a storybook (SpongeBob receives a technical manual to read—without pictures), having his boo-boo kissed, and naptime. Meanwhile, Grandma—superbly voiced by actress Marion Ross, who played Mrs. Cunningham on the series *Happy Days*—offers her grandson a more adultlike dish in the form of steamed coral. Yuck!

Finally, a frustrated SpongeBob cries, "I don't want to grow up. . . . I want kissy-kissy on my boo-boo," says the conflicted sponge. That's when Grandma's advice sets everything right. "You don't have to be a baby to get old Grandma's love. . . . No matter how grown up you get, you will always be my little baby-boo. And remember, you can kiss your Grandma and still be an adult," she says, giving him a cookie.

"Ah, Grandma, could you not mention this to the guys down at the Krusty Krab?" asks SpongeBob.

"No problem," she answers as the pair embrace.

That's when the sound of laughter creeps in—for the audience's ears only—as the crowd from the Krusty Krab, gathered outside of Grandma's window, takes in the entire scene.

BENEATH THE SURFACE

The episode "Grandma's Kisses" examines the premise of youngsters walking that line between childhood and adolescence. It's obvious that there is no roadmap (sorry, GPS) for the journey, and having one foot over the line into new territory doesn't banish your desire for sources of comfort from an earlier, familiar one.

SHARING A SENSE OF HUMOR

When Patrick joins SpongeBob's boating class, teacher Mrs. Puff asks the newbie to share his name with his fellow classmates in "New Student Starfish" (season 3, episode 13). Patrick, feeling the public pressure, freezes in front of the class. Finally, he blurts out, "Twenty-four." There's a roar of laughter among the students, with Mrs. Puff muttering to herself, "Oh, great. Another genius." Patrick sits down next to SpongeBob, chuckling over his own response before quietly repeating it to his best friend, as if sharing a private joke. They both snicker. Then SpongeBob says in a hushed tone, "I've thought of something funnier than twenty-four." "Let me hear it," counters Patrick. "Twenty-five," says SpongeBob, as the pair do all they can to contain their surging laughter. The eons that their distant relatives spent together from the primordial ooze to today must have perfectly aligned their senses of humor.

Note to the reader: If you're thinking about saying "twenty-six" out loud, you'd better closely examine your own family tree.

QUIZ QUESTION 9

Of the foursome that includes SpongeBob's paternal grandparents and parents, only one of them doesn't wear glasses. Which is the character who isn't bespectacled?

The answer can be found after the book's conclusion.

BUBBLE TIME

In *SpongeBob SquarePants*, air bubbles are omnipresent. They're often used by Stephen Hillenburg to signal a change in scenes, momentarily obscuring our view as they fill the screen before rising to the surface. The creator also uses air bubbles to subtly remind the audience that we're all underwater yet somehow breathing, whether that's though the magic of animation or a scuba air tank.

But SpongeBob himself, however, has an affinity for a different kind of bubble—a soap bubble. They even spell out his name during the animation sequence for the opening theme song before popping. In the second episode of the series, "Bubblestand," SpongeBob gives both Patrick and Squidward lessons in the art of blowing soap bubbles. Many audience members have probably experienced this at science museums around the country. But the über-talented sponge, using a simple bubble wand, takes bubble blowing to a new level. He blows bubbles resembling a flock of ducks, a perfect cube, a sea centipede, a boat, and an elephant, which even trumpets when it eventually pops.

Professional bubble artists actually create soap bubbles in different shapes, including cubes and tetrahedrons (a three-dimensional shape with four triangular faces). They can even put people, smoke, and helium inside their bubbles. The idea of creating soap bubbles as a form of play began in the late nineteenth century when England's Pears Soap Company started marketing a soapy solution and a bubble pipe as amusement for children. But the hollow spheres with the iridescent surface have serious science behind them. They are a reflection of a mathematical equation concerning minimal surface. Each bubble naturally assumes the shape that will enclose a given volume of air using the least surface area possible. So soap bubbles are masters of efficiency. And when a pair of bubbles merge, they adopt a shape that makes their surface area as small as possible to hold their combined volume of air.

In the second season's third episode, titled "Bubble Buddy," SpongeBob takes his talents to a new level. With no one to keep him company on a particular afternoon, SpongeBob tries to invent a friend. He fruitlessly cycles through Stick Buddy, Rock Buddy, and Sink Buddy, who runs too hot and cold to be a good companion. Our protagonist turns to the magic of his bubble wand and creates Bubble Buddy, a life-size bubble figure. Though Bubble Buddy mostly remains silent, together the pair have lunch at the Krusty Krab, where Bubble Buddy pays the bill (in bubble money, mind you) before they hold up the line for the Port-o-Head at Goo Lagoon where the bubble figure needs to relieve himself (have patience; it's his first time in the bathroom alone). Bikini Bottomites lose their temper with the mute and seemingly inanimate Bubble Buddy and attempt to pop him with sharp pins. That's when SpongeBob passionately defends his new friend.

"He's not just a bubble! He's a bubble buddy!" exclaims SpongeBob. He's my friend and I love him. Haven't you ever had a very special friend?"

The crowd recounts their own relationships with inanimate objects from a nickel to a muffler to piece of jerky. But they still want to pop Bubble Buddy, who eventually speaks up for himself. "Hey, don't I get a say in this?" asks the iridescent figure, physically stopping the first pin thrust toward him. "I'll see you later, SpongeBob. It's getting a little weird around here."

Then Bubble Buddy appropriately hails a bubble taxicab before being driven away to safety.

"Seems like only this morning I held his bottle," says a teary-eyed SpongeBob after his creation's departure. "They blow up so fast."

FAN FORUM

"SpongeBob is filled with bright colors and the unknown. He has an eagerness to him that people don't usually have, and optimism. *SpongeBob* is my childhood, sitting in front of the TV just in time for it to start. It was the only time that I truly watched television."—V. S.

INDELIBLE STATEMENTS

Once, tattoos representing the seafaring life embodied images of pirate ships flying the Jolly Roger (skull-and-crossbones flag), anchors (like Popeye's), lighthouses, and mermaid-like sirens singing upon jagged rocks above the tide. Today, however, there's a new wave of tattoos boasting the wearer's devotion to the sea and their favorite animated series. One of them is actually a split-level, fully furnished pineapple.

SpongeBob SquarePants-inspired tattoos have become quite common, often serving as an individual's first tattoo experience. Those who want SpongeBob inked on them might be making the statement that they are happy, carefree, and childlike in their view of the world around them and all the immense positives it has to offer. A best friends forever or BFF tattoo usually includes an image SpongeBob and Patrick enjoying life together. Wall Street types might be drawn to Mr. Krabs, displaying his love of money. Those who want to prove how tough and resilient they are might choose a tattoo of Sandy Cheeks in extreme sports mode, whereas individuals desiring to challenge a large and unyielding world could opt for an image of Plankton. Teachers might gravitate toward a tattoo of Mrs. Puff. Love animals? Then you might be the perfect candidate for a Gary tattoo.

For fans younger than the legal age of consent, there are always temporary tattoos to either express your love of the series or make a personal statement about yourself.

ANIMATED INK

Stephen Hillenburg and the writers give us an up-close look at tattoos in Bikini Bottom, working them into the plotline for "No Weenies Allowed" (season 3, episode 8). SpongeBob wants entrance, along with Sandy, to the Salty Spittoon, a club that allows only the roughest, toughest patrons inside. How tough? Eating a bowl of nails for breakfast won't cut it, not unless you have it without milk. Guarding the entrance to the club is Big Reg, who sports a tattoo on his chest with the word "Mom" in its center. Sandy shows him how tough she is by ripping the tattoo completely off Big Reg and then putting it back upside down, with it reading, "Wow." Later in the episode, a patron looking for admittance has a tattoo of a sea monster on one arm, and he can make it dance by flexing. That's when Big Reg notices the SpongeBob tattoo on the patron's other arm. But it's really SpongeBob himself trying to sneak past. Could that have been the first SpongeBob tattoo ever?

What could cause Mr. Krabs to give himself a tattoo, right at the register of the Krusty Krab? Why, a customer ordering one of everything on the menu. SpongeBob's soap bubble creation did that, so Mr. Krabs tattooed the name "Bubble Buddy" in an arrowed heart across his chest. I think that relationship moved too fast. How about you?

10

MRS. PUFF

THANK YOU, NICK

The character of driving school instructor Mrs. Puff, voiced by Mary Jo Catlett, was not in Stephen Hillenburg's original pitch bible. The idea of bringing a teacher into the cast of characters evolved from Nickelodeon's insistence that the main protagonist Sponge Boy/SpongeBob attend school, in order to have something in common with the network's target audience. Hillenburg's remedy for this wasn't to put SpongeBob in a traditional all-day school setting, which would have both pinned down the character's age and seriously curtailed his time at the Krusty Krab and other Bikini Bottom venues. Instead, the creator opted for a weekly (more or less) boating school, with the premise that SpongeBob, no matter how hard he or Mrs. Puff tries, simply can't pass the exam to receive his boating license—the equivalent to our driver's license.

Mrs. Puff, a porcupine/pufferfish, vows—despite her own intense frustration and detriment—"I pledge that as long as a student is willing to learn, I shall never give up." An instant after uttering those words, Mrs.

Puff meets the student who will change her life. "Hi. I'm SpongeBob SquarePants," says our porous protagonist in a ray-of-sunshine voice.

How has Mrs. Puff gotten to Bikini Bottom? That's a loaded question and one that casts a small yet intriguing shadow on her background. When assessing SpongeBob's failures and the damage his bad driving has caused, Mrs. Puff says to herself, "I'll have to move to a new city. Start a new boating school with a new name. No. Not again." *Again?*

And what happened to her husband, Mr. Puff? All Hillenburg and the writers will confirm is that he's currently a lamp fixture in someone's surface home.

After taking responsibility for SpongeBob's disastrous driving, could sweet but mysterious Mrs. Puff, who seems to adjust to life behind bars in the Bikini Bottom jail quite easily—"I like it here, these are my people"— have had something to do with SpongeBob's disappearance? Did she push him toward the hooks? *Nah. Probably not.* But the fact that Hillenburg leaves all of these intriguing questions floating makes her character even more delightful.

To put it plainly, Mrs. Puff suffers due to SpongeBob's failures during his boating exams. He aces the oral section of the exam every time. It's the practical part that tightens his nerves and causes him to freeze up, usually with disastrous driving consequences.

When pulling out of a parking spot during one of his exams, Mrs. Puff, who wisely wears a crash helmet, asks SpongeBob what to do next after starting the boat. "Floor it?" he nervously replies, a moment prior to their high-speed crash. Their many crashes precede Mrs. Puff's signature moment—when she puffs up with air like a vehicle's airbag upon impact and complains, "Oh, SpongeBob!"

Near the end of the fourth season, the episode "Driven to Tears" (episode 17) informs us that SpongeBob has failed his boating test fifty-eight times. Earlier that season, however, an administrator from the Boating Association, who shows up to suspend Mrs. Puff's teaching credentials in "Mrs. Puff, You're Fired" (episode 9), claims that SpongeBob has failed a hyperbolic 1,258,056 times. That's too much bad driving to be true.

After SpongeBob's misadventures behind the wheel unravel the new teacher, Mrs. Puff is reinstated.

Undeterred by his previous failures, SpongeBob sentences his pufferfish instructor to a seemingly unlimited horizon of future crashes together. "Sorry I'm unteachable. . . . I promise it won't take me a million tries this time."

If that were only true.

SIDESTEPPING THE SYSTEM

During the premiere season's "Boating School" (episode 4), SpongeBob unwittingly attempts to cheat on his exam by having Patrick radio him driving instructions via an antenna concealed beneath his unusually tall hat. It's working beautifully until SpongeBob recognizes his wrongdoing and begins to cry, veering off the road. Mrs. Puff responds: "It's quite alright. You can cheat. . . . Cheat that way!" pointing him toward the driving course's finish line. But, alas, another crash and another failure.

By the time the second season of the series is in full swing, it's no more "Mrs. Patience" for the pufferfish in "No Free Rides" (episode 10). The instructor realizes more serious measures are required. "There's only one way out," contemplates an exasperated Mrs. Puff. "A teacher's ace in the hole—extra credit."

After writing a ten-word essay in which Mrs. Puff gives SpongeBob the first seven words, "What I learned in boating school is . . . ," the student receives his license. Naturally, it isn't that easy. SpongeBob hilariously suffers through writer's block, hand cramps, and other maladies before the short assignment is marked official. But he does it, and Mrs. Puff announces: "You pass!"

Of course, SpongeBob has some reservations about the process. "Mrs. Puff, I don't feel like I really did anything," contemplates SpongeBob.

"That's the way extra credit is supposed to feel," counters Mrs. Puff.

The teacher suffers second thoughts about turning the erratic driver loose on the citizens of Bikini Bottom, too. But it's okay because Sponge-Bob doesn't own a boat to drive. That's when his parents visit and give their son a new boat as a graduation present. Now Mrs. Puff's conscience is in full regret mode. So she dresses up as a masked thief and tries to steal SpongeBob's new ride in the middle of the night.

The boat's already in motion when SpongeBob confronts the still-unknown perpetrator. "Who are you and what are you doing in my boat? And why are you wearing that ski mask, because you're not skiing," asks an angry SpongeBob. "I know who you are."

Does SpongeBob recognize Mrs. Puff? Not on your life.

"You're a boat-jacker," says SpongeBob.

The pair struggle for control of the boat on a wild ride through a field of giant snapping clams, a field of sharp cheese graters (remember, Hillenburg gave SpongeBob pants so he wouldn't be confused with a block of cheese), and finally through a vast field of educational television—a perfect jab by the *SpongeBob SquarePants* writers at their perceived critics.

Once her true identity is exposed (sans the mask), Mrs. Puff apologizes to SpongeBob for improperly passing him as she sits in the Bikini Bottom Jail, and SpongeBob returns his boating license.

Her one chance at an early parole? Giving the warden free driving lessons.

BENEATH THE SURFACE

As with all of the episodes in which SpongeBob fails his boating exam, the message is subtle and consistent. SpongeBob never stops reaching for what he hopes to achieve. The failures, instead of devastating him, give him more resolve to pass the next time around. It's a valuable model for perseverance.

QUIZ QUESTION 10

Here's another two-parter: (1) The boat given to SpongeBob by his parents had a vanity license plate. What did it say? (2) There have been several driver's licenses displayed throughout the series, providing characters' dates of birth and addresses. Let's focus on those addresses for a moment. What's the zip code for Bikini Bottom?

The answer can be found after the book's conclusion.

LOVE BIRDS

Ever since Mrs. Puff walked into the Krusty Krab for lunch in "Krusty Love" (season 2, episode 16), she has been the object of Mr. Krabs's affections. Krabs even spends money on her during a series of dates, so you know he's serious. That is, until Mrs. Puff demands to pay her fair share and "go Dutch," touching Mr. Krabs's frugal heart even more deeply. The poetic Mr. Krabs also has a slew of endearing terms for her, including "my little shrimp boat" and "my beautiful bell buoy."

HISTORICAL REFERENCE POINT

Looking at the bright side of being in jail, Mrs. Puff begins to tell Sponge-Bob, "I won't have to deal with *you*." Realizing that SpongeBob's feelings will be hurt, she pulls up on the single syllable of "you," transforming it into "U . . . uranium in the water supply." Mrs. Puff spared SpongeBob's feelings, while Hillenburg and the writers commented on the lingering effects of the past's nuclear experiments in Bikini Atoll.

Brilliantly done!

CHAPTER 10

PERSPECTIVE: TOM KENNY

Q: What do your own kids think about you being the voice of SpongeBob?

TK: I have two children, a son who is twenty-five and a daughter who is nineteen, so neither one of them grew up in a pre-SpongeBob period. I always felt gratified when they were watching the show because they were really into it. They weren't thinking about me, about how the voice of SpongeBob and Gary belonged to their father, who may have been washing dishes in the kitchen. Instead, they were immersed in the show, rooting for that funny yellow sponge and his pink starfish friend. The combination of its elements—the animation, writing, and music—were so strong that even if they lived with the guy who did the main character's voice, they were glued to what was happening on the screen.

11

PLANKTON

LOOK DOWN

What's a comedic community, whether on the surface or beneath the waves, without a pint-sized antagonist boasting a Napoleon complex—feelings of inferiority due to one's short stature? In fact, the character of Sheldon J. Plankton, a tiny, one-eyed planktonic copepod voiced by Douglas Lawrence Osowski (aka Mr. Lawrence), probably would consider "pint-sized" a compliment, or at least a step up in the world.

Plankton is Bikini Bottom's resident villain and proprietor of the Chum Bucket, a nearly customer-less rival of the Krusty Krab, situated directly across the street. The Chum Bucket, whose parent company is Sheldon Plankton Enterprises, a Division of No Fun Incorporated, first opened on the same day that Eugene Krabs launched the Krusty Krab. Not particularly known for his business acumen (that's being kind), Plankton is also a scientist and inventor who enjoys reminding others, "I went to college." Maybe he went to SMU. No, not Southern Methodist University in Texas, but rather, Short and Maniacal University.

Unfortunately, it's difficult for Plankton to maintain a high profile when he's literally underfoot. In defeat, which is constant, Plankton often goes *splat* beneath someone's foot or via a flyswatter. He can also be flicked several hundred yards away with just two fingers. But that doesn't stop him from dreaming big.

Plankton's announced objective is to steal Mr. Krabs's secret krabby patty formula, though it's fairly obvious that acquiring a few friends might easily quell the single-cell protozoan's need to act out. Ironically, Plankton and Krabs were best friends at Poseidon Elementary School, until the two most unpopular kids on the undersea playground conceived the idea of outdoing the local burger joint, Stinky Burgers, with their own burger-like creation to gain money, popularity, and power.

In the fifth season's "Friend or Foe" (episode 1), the adolescent pair split over culinary creative differences. Mr. Krabs then lucks into a better-tasting burger formula by accident when several unnamed ingredients slide from a falling shelf into a vat of burger mix. That was the creation Eugene Krabs would call a krabby patty. The criteria for early success by not-so-discriminating palates were that it was "edible" and had "flavor." Oh, and there was one more important attribute: "We can actually hold it down," praised a non-vomiting customer.

Looking back at their journey together, Plankton says, "All the years I was trying to steal your formula, I was really trying to steal back our friendship." Of course, a moment later he tries to swipe the formula while hugging Krabs. That's so Plankton!

QUIZ QUESTION 11

In which unsavory venue did young Sheldon Plankton and Eugene Krabs open their first burger stand together as friends?

The answer can be found after the book's conclusion.

TRADING PLACES

In "The Algae's Always Greener" (season 3, episode 1), Plankton trades places with Mr. Krabs through his invention called the Life Switcher. But Plankton quickly realizes the new and difficult challenges of living as Mr. Krabs. SpongeBob, who gave a customer a large soda instead of the medium he had ordered, is driving Plankton (now the boss of the Krusty Krab) crazy with one of his meltdowns. An insistent Pearl, who sees Plankton as her dad, wants a steep advance on her allowance. He also has to deal with a naked Mr. Krabs, playing his former role and trying to steal the secret krabby patty formula. At the height of the vice-versa insanity, Plankton just wants his old life back and leaves. "Goodbye, everyone. I'll see you all in my therapy," he says.

HORRIBLE, TERRIBLE SECRET

Sheldon Plankton finally gets his minute hands on the secret krabby patty formula in "Plankton's Army" (season 3, episode 18). "A pinch of salt, three teaspoons of chopped onions, a cup of love—mixed together with the most important ingredient of all—four heaping pounds of freshly ground plankton." Upon hearing the news, a horrified Sheldon runs off, screaming in fright. It's reminiscent of a scene in the sci-fi show *The Twilight Zone* when aliens arrive on earth with a book titled *To Serve Man*. Then the humans discover that it's actually a cookbook.

Don't be too grossed out. Mr. Krabs planted that faux formula for Plankton to find. *Psst.* Krabs keeps the real formula hidden under his mattress, at least during this episode.

PERFECT RELATIONSHIP

Stephen Hillenburg put Plankton in the perfect relationship, one with a computer wife named Karen, who technically doesn't have a heart. She's a Mark II Surplus UNIVAC with 256 gigabytes of random access memory, and they've been together since Plankton built her in grade school. She is always reminding Plankton of the various plans he devised but forgot to implement, including the infamous Plan Z from *The SpongeBob SquarePants Movie* (2004). But she's equally willing to cut him down to size with her sharp wit whenever he screws up. Karen is voiced by Jill Talley, who is the real-life wife of Tom Kenny. And Karen is named for Stephen Hillenburg's wife, Karen. So the personal connections for the computerized character abound.

JOUSTING AT BLISS

Karen may be hardwired, but she certainly has feelings and boundaries. In season ten's "Plankton Gets the Boot" (episode 4), Karen lovingly calls her single-cell husband "Planky-bear" and is fishing for a compliment about her new screensaver. But the domination-driven Plankton is too busy with one of his impending schemes to pay any attention to her personal needs. In frustration, he blurts out, "Your new screensaver is stupid. It makes your processor look fat!" That's when Karen immediately stands up for herself (wait, she's always standing, isn't she?) and boots Plankton out of the Chum Bucket. So Plankton goes to stay with SpongeBob at the pineapple.

"I'm sorry Karen threw you out," says SpongeBob.

"Threw me out? I threw her in!" objects Plankton.

SpongeBob gives Plankton lessons in being nice and even disguises himself as a female robot in an attempt to make Karen jealous when the pair visit the Chum Bucket. Karen is actually touched by Plankton's plan to get her back. But their romantic reunion is short-lived when Plankton insults her again.

"My motherboard was right about you. She warned me about you. And I should have listened," says Karen, as she and Plankton resume their rather antagonistic relationship.

Though Karen herself doesn't eat, she is responsible for cooking at the Chum Bucket, which opened the same day as the Krusty Krab. She makes Plankton special meals like chum pot pie and holographic meatloaf. *Holographic?* Sure. How else might a computer imagine eating? Still, Plankton, who struggles with the concept of taking personal responsibility for his failures, seems to forever be shifting the blame onto Karen, causing her to leave in "Komputer Overload" (season 6, episode 15). Her farewell note reads: "I can't go into sleep-mode at night knowing that you'll continue to blame me for all of your failures."

Winning Karen back, Plankton tells her, "I could never replace you, honeybunch." But just two seasons later, Plankton builds a replacement wife in "Karen 2.0" (season 8, episode 19). It's an episode in which Karen actually goes to work in the Krusty Krab. You didn't think Mr. Krabs would turn down an unpaid robot employee, did you? But in the end, Karen destroys Karen 2.0 after her replacement accidentally rolls over and flattens Plankton, a situation he's been in many times before. That reunites our acidic and bickering couple—protozoan and machine—in their combative relationship.

THE WEDDING PICTURE

Every now and then, just so Karen can't deny it, Plankton needs to get out their wedding picture. What's so special about the photo? Plankton lovingly holds Karen's plug in both hands, but that's not it. Seems that on the day they were wed, Plankton sported a bushy mustache and a full head of wavy black hair. Who would have guessed?

FOOLING SOME OF THE FISH SOME OF THE TIME

A lack of business at the Chum Bucket is nothing new for Plankton. In fact, it's standard operating procedure. But when Karen smartly suggests that he advertise his fare—an idea that Plankton quickly claims as his own—Plankton begins to ponder the proper strategy in the episode "Chum Bucket Supreme" (season 6, episode 22). On the sign out front, he puts up the slogan: "Chum Is Metabolic Fuel." Patrick sees it, and his brain literally melts down trying to decipher the word "metabolic."

"These words make my head sad," says Patrick, the Everyman (uh, Every-aquatic) of Bikini Bottom. "I don't get it."

So Patrick rearranges the letters on the sign to read: "Chum Is Fum" (that's right, *F-U-M*).

In response, there's suddenly a huge line of aquatics waiting to eat at the Chum Bucket, which is known for its poor-tasting and unhealthy food. All because of Patrick's slogan. Now what does that say about the gullibility of Bikini Bottomites? Are Stephen Hillenburg and the writing staff saying that real-life people are influenced by the seemingly senseless advertising of various fast-food chains?

COURTROOM DRAMA

When Plankton sues Mr. Krabs in court for slipping on SpongeBob's freshly mopped floor inside the Krusty Krab, Hillenburg and the writers lean on some contemporary media markers. The music playing in the background as the litigants, Plankton and Mr. Krabs, enter the proceedings is the opening strains of the theme music from the TV reality show *The People's Court*. The judge also resembles and speaks like Judge Judith Sheindlin of another reality show, *Judge Judy*. As a social comment on the perceived money-based motivation of some personal injury lawyers (often referred to as ambulance chasers), the writers appropriately selected the name Richard A. Bottomfeeder for the lawyer representing Mr. Krabs.

EARLY LOVE

When Stephen Hillenburg founded his own Los Angeles–based production company in 1998, he named it United Plankton Pictures, showing the future series character some early love. By the way, real-life blue whales can consume up to sixteen tons of plankton in a single day, normally by opening their mouth and swimming through a huge "cloud" of tiny plankton. Our Sheldon J. Plankton would prefer that you keep that dietary fact a secret from Pearl Krabs!

12

HERE, THERE, EVERYWHERE

THE FIRST FEATURE FILM

The SpongeBob SquarePants Movie, a live-action/animated film based on Stephen Hillenburg's cast of crazy characters, debuted in theaters to rave reviews by both fans of the Nickelodeon series and first-time "Bobbers" in 2004.

Epic journeys are often punctuated by a quest. There's Sir Galahad's quest for the Holy Grail, Aeneas's quest for a homeland, and Jason and the Argonauts' search for the Golden Fleece. In their film, Hillenburg and the writers give a wink and a nod to those great mythical quests by sending SpongeBob and Patrick on their own rite-of-passage journey to return Neptune's stolen crown and to mature in the process.

The film opens with a dream sequence in which SpongeBob is now the manager of the Krusty Krab. The situation is critical. Life in Bikini Bottom has come to a screeching halt as a customer sits alone in the restaurant, distraught because his krabby patty with cheese has no cheese. The authorities can conceive of only one potential solution: employ the very best there ever was at a fast-food fix up, an absolute patty legend.

SpongeBob struts inside wearing monogrammed boots and the confidence of a big-time bomb defuser. Naturally, SpongeBob saves the day by delicately laying a slice of cheese upon the open-faced patty. (Well, it is his dream.)

In animated reality, Mr. Krabs is opening the Krusty Krab II, ironically, right next to the original Krusty Krab. The entire town has turned out for the grand opening and Mr. Krabs's announcement of the new store's manager.

"The new manager is a hardworking, loyal employee. . . . The obvious choice for the job, a name you all know, starts with an *S*," says Mr. Krabs, while SpongeBob squirms in his seat in the audience, ready to explode, waiting to hear his name.

That's when Mr. Krabs sets the film's premise in motion.

"Squidward Tentacles," announces Mr. Krabs. Squidward's face is aghast in shock.

A clueless SpongeBob sprints up to the stage to accept the position that he believes he was awarded.

SpongeBob believes he's about to be named manager of the Krusty Krab II. *Paramount/ Photofest © Paramount Pictures*

"People of Bikini Bottom, as the manager I'll—," begins SpongeBob before Mr. Krabs interrupts him and whispers into his ear.

"I'm making a complete what of myself?" SpongeBob responds into the microphone, announcing the hushed conversation to the crowd.

Listen hard enough and you can hear Krabs faintly whisper the word "jackass."

After some reflection, Mr. Krabs says, "You're just a kid. To be a manager you have to be a man. Otherwise they'd call it 'kid-ager.' Do you understand-ager?"

SpongeBob is crushed and now focuses on becoming what others perceive to be a "man." Will SpongeBob rise to some sort of incredible challenge? Will his fantasies of saving the day become a fictional reality? Well, it's his movie and he'll receive every chance to expand (sponge humor) in front of our eyes.

Hold tight and pass the popcorn. The perfect setup is coming.

When Plankton steals Neptune's crown, which ends up in a surface-world curio shop named Shell City, the free will of most of Bikini Bottom via a mind control device, it's up to SpongeBob and Patrick to save the day.

The ensuing comedy is madcap as Neptune's mermaid daughter gives SpongeBob and Patrick seaweed mustaches to convince them of their manhood. They also tour the ocean in a krabby-patty-shaped boat named "patty," using a spatula for a starter key. Its license plate is perfect for a food delivery vehicle: 2-GO.

In true epic fashion, our aspiring heroic pair encounters a dreaded "cyclops"—a live-action diver wearing a snorkel mask, hence the illusion of one big eye. Abducted by the cyclops, they are taken to Shell City, where they find the stolen crown. But they become dehydrated under a heat lamp used to dry out a store full of abducted sea creatures destined to be sold as souvenirs. (This will make you think twice before purchasing a starfish or other trinket at a seaside gift shop.) Their tears, however, short-circuit the lamp, causing the sprinkler system to turn on, reviving them and all the other sea creatures.

On the beach, escaping with the crown, SpongeBob and Patrick are rescued by actor David Hasselhoff, who played a lifeguard on the TV series *Baywatch*. "The Hoff" aids their return to Bikini Bottom, where SpongeBob uses his musical creativity to go full-on guitar wizard, releasing everyone from Plankton's mind control through the power of rock and roll.

Since our hero has shed the role of "kid," guess who Mr. Krabs names as his new "*man*-ager"?

No. Not Patrick. Silly.

The film triumphantly brings SpongeBob to the big screen.

COLORFUL CHARACTER

Pantone is an industry color guide widely used by artists, designers, printers, manufacturers, and marketers throughout the world to accurately identify how characters and products should be colored for consistency. So if you want to draw a picture of SpongeBob, there are some exact colors you might want to use. Because of the character's popularity, Pantone actually has named a color SpongeBob Yellow. You know you've hit it big when they name a color for you. Maybe next we'll find him in the Crayola box. SpongeBob's pores are shaded a light olive green, and his eyes are Pacific blue to match the animated background of the blue waters of the Pacific Ocean. We hope that's not being too *S-pacific* for you!

SOUNDING IT OUT

Ever recognize the impending entrance of one of your favorite *SpongeBob SquarePants* characters before they appear onscreen? That's probably because you know the sound of their footsteps. In filmmaking and other types of media, the term "Foley" is used to describe the reproduction of everyday sounds and the adding of sound effects. It's named for sound effect artist Jack Foley (1891–1967), who produced the sound effects for many famous films, from *The Phantom of the Opera* (1925) to *Dracula* (1931) to *Spartacus* (1960).

SpongeBob's footsteps are normally a light squeaking sound, as compared to the higher-pitched squeak used in the episode "Squeaky Boots." Squidward's footsteps are the sound of suction cups. Remember, he walks on four feet, so that effect is quadrupled.

Search your memory. Consider these characters: Patrick, Mr. Krabs, Pearl, and Plankton. How would you describe the sound of their footsteps?

FAMILIAR FISH

You *know* that you've seen that fish before. He's a brown grouper with light brown fins and large black eyes. His most common form of dress is brown pants and a black belt. Well, you're correct. That incidental background fish has appeared in dozens and dozens of episodes. He's even had several speaking parts. The writers finally gave him a name to identify that fish among themselves. Congratulations! You're very observant. That fish is named Fred.

PERSPECTIVE: PAUL VOLPONI

I was working with a group of high school students in Watertown, Connecticut, teaching a creative writing workshop. I had four names projected on a screen: Peter Parker, Kim Kardashian, Woodrow Wilson, and SpongeBob SquarePants. My question to the group was, "What do the four names have in common?" It was a quick lesson on the value of alliteration. But before I got to that point, I asked the students to explain who each of those four individuals were.

I could see the restrained excitement on a student's face in the front row as I made my way through the list in order. As soon as we had finished speaking about the third name, former US president Woodrow Wilson, that student couldn't hold back her excitement any longer. Her hand shot into the air and she said, "Paul, pick me. Please. I have to do the next one. I just have to!" I asked for her name. "Maria," she said hurriedly before blurting out, "You want to know the next name? I'll tell you. SpongeBob is a god to me. He's the greatest character ever. Look at this," she continued, pulling up the pant legs of her jeans to reveal a pair of socks with a smiling SpongeBob waving a jellyfishing net on them.

I had a co-teacher, Jim Nenopoulos, working with me that day with whom I had worked for many years. Before Jim became a teacher, he'd had a long career as a standup comedian, and he is close friends with Tom Kenny, the voice of SpongeBob. I hadn't realized it, but Jim snuck out into the hallway with his cell phone and called Tom Kenny after hearing about Maria's admiration for the character.

In his haste to do a good deed, Jim forgot about the time difference between coasts. It was 8:30 a.m. in Connecticut, but it was only 5:30 a.m. in California, where Kenny lived. I wasn't personally on the line to hear it, but Jim tells me that Kenny only picked up the phone because he thought somebody might have died. Why else would Jim be calling him at that time?

Jim told Kenny, "No. It's nothing like that. I have a student here who's a big fan of yours." Jim said that Kenny verbally hammered him for almost two minutes with some intermittent language that would undoubtedly be considered off-limits for the saintly cartoon character he voiced. But when that initial wave of annoyance passed, Kenny performed as SpongeBob for the class via speakerphone for a solid five minutes, answering questions and performing many of his most memorable lines. Kudos to Tom and Jim for making that day one that Maria will never forget.

QUIZ QUESTION 12

Is SpongeBob right-handed or left-handed? Bonus points for any additional information concerning that answer.

The answer can be found after the book's conclusion.

LET'S PLAY

SpongeBob SquarePants merchandise, which includes clothing, jewelry, toys, games, and a host of knickknacks (Mr. Krabs would be proud), has become nearly omnipresent in our society. You never know exactly where you'll see a yellow smiling face, two huge teeth, and a pair of warm and welcoming eyes waiting to greet you.

There are blankets, bedsheets, and pillowcases adorned with the characters. Plushes and pillows—especially ones shaped like SpongeBob, Patrick, Gary, and Pearl—wait for someone with whom they can softly cuddle. What fan of Sandy Cheeks wouldn't want to own a treedome snow globe? Wouldn't any starstruck goldfish want a replica of SpongeBob's pineapple, Squidward's Easter Island head home, or the Krusty Krab sitting at the bottom of their aquarium blowing air bubbles?

Series-inspired finger puppets, beanies, and paint sets allow you to create your own Bikini Bottom adventures. You can place padded *ka-rah-tay* hands on a SpongeBob action figure and chop away to your heart's content. Sea flower pendants dangle from the necks of fans, while a Plankton key chain might put up a worthy argument about not being stuffed back down into the darkness of your pocket. Do it anyway!

You can probably close your eyes and envision Patrick's trunks—lime green and decorated with purple sea flowers. Well, you can buy a pair just like them, both online and in stores, then hit the beach with the same fun-loving attitude as Patrick Star. Just be careful about actually *hitting* the beach—it just might hit back in the form of a crashing wave. And no, the beach is not where *sand*wiches come from.

What's another way to cool off on a hot summer day? Ice cream (or, as Sandy would say, "frozen cow juice") trucks supply SpongeBob SquarePants Popsicle bars. A nearly exact replica of the character, it is fruit punch and cotton candy flavored. Its large black eye pupils are actually gumballs, so it's two treats in one. In a second-season episode titled "The Smoking Peanut" (episode 12), Patrick takes a healthy lick of a SpongeBob-like yellow ice pop. Perhaps that was the inspiration for this confectionary. Of course, once the ice pop begins to melt, you end up with a distorted and sometimes scary representation of the character on a stick.

Talking about scary, there are Halloween costumes depicting several of the characters. Some trick-or-treaters and Halloween party revelers add their own personal touches to their otherwise innocuous costumes with blood and accessories such as maces and chainsaws. But perhaps the most macabre series-inspired product on the market is SpongeBob SkullPants, an action figure with no skin on its face, five large teeth (two top, three bottom), and no eyes in its sockets. If you like horror movies and SpongeBob, this might be the toy for you.

Let's not forget about the remote-controlled cars and boats with SpongeBob at the wheel. There's even one shaped like the Patty Mobile (a vehicle with a krabby patty design) from *The SpongeBob SquarePants Movie*. Remember to stay at the controls—SpongeBob still doesn't have his valid license.

If all of that playing leaves you with an appetite, you do have options. There's a yellow SpongeBob slow cooker that can simmer meals during the course of the day. No fish or crabs, please. And for those of you who like to start your morning off with a bright smile, there is a yellow SpongeBob toaster that imprints each slice of bread or bagel with the character's happy face. The toaster's sales slogan? "I'm Bready." No, I didn't make that up.

13

SOCIAL RELEVANCE

BENEATH THE SURFACE

Here is a trio of brilliantly written and performed episodes that address the struggles of school-age children, preteens, and teens in our society at large, proving that Stephen Hillenburg's underwater community is not so different from ours. The creator and writers tackle the subjects of identity, bullying, and hurtful humor played out against a comical background, encouraging us not to back away from these all-too-real and sensitive issues.

AM I STILL ME?

Adolescents often struggle with trying to understand who they are and maintaining a clear sense of identity. A third-season episode titled "Missing Identity" (episode 18) follows SpongeBob through a day of self-doubt after losing his Krusty Krab nametag. The episode opens late at night in a near-empty and dilapidated diner. SpongeBob enters ready to tell his tale of woe to the waitress and a lone customer sitting at the counter. "I lost something once. I lost something I couldn't live without, my identity," says SpongeBob, as if he'd just stepped into a 1950s black-and-white movie, complete with a haunting soundtrack of a single alto saxophone in the background.

In flashbacks, we witness the day in question unfold, with a caveat from our protagonist to the impatient pair at the diner that "a great story can't be rushed."

A new customer to the Krusty Krab reminds SpongeBob that he really should wear his nametag. In response, he points at the place on his square shirt where it always resides. But it's gone. Deep down, SpongeBob knows who he is—a caring friend to all who call Bikini Bottom home and an ace fry cook. Still, he begins to comically stress over his nametag's whereabouts and to subtly worry about maintaining his identity without it.

"My nametag is out there somewhere, lost and hungry," he cries before imagining a nightmarish vision of a crook prominently wearing it while robbing the First Nautical Bank.

Mr. Krabs announces that there will be a uniform inspection in an hour, and the pressure on SpongeBob's square shoulders intensifies. Squidward suggests that SpongeBob retrace his steps that day. With a nod to the hilarious film *Groundhog Day* (1993), Hillenburg and the writing staff make SpongeBob relive his day over and over, including a slapstick fall down the steps of his pineapple and a taste test of Gary's snail food. And thanks to Patrick being unable to remember his one key line—"Hi, SpongeBob"—SpongeBob keeps stopping and then restarting the sequence to get it exactly correct. Hooray, Pat.

Eventually, SpongeBob and Patrick go dumpster diving to look for the nametag in the trash. That's when Patrick discovers that SpongeBob, in a hurry to get dressed that morning, put his shirt on backward.

"I know where your nametag is," says Patrick, looking at his best friend from behind. "Where?" says SpongeBob, turning to face him. Patrick instantly forgets what he's seen. Several literal back-and-forths later, the pair solves the comedic quandary with one minute to go before Mr. Krabs's uniform inspection.

Back at the diner in real time, SpongeBob reads the waitress's nametag and calls her "Betty." She replies, "I'm not Betty. I borrowed a uniform while mine's at the cleaners."

Bravo, Not-Betty!

DEALING WITH A BULLY

At one time or another, almost every student has had to confront a school bully, usually accompanied by intense feelings of uneasiness. Well, Stephen Hillenburg wants you to know that SpongeBob is no different and that you absolutely have that experience in common with him.

When Mrs. Puff introduces Flats the Flounder as the new student at her driving school in "The Bully" (season 3, episode 3), he casually informs his classmates that "I like to kick people's butts." And by "people," he means cartoon fish and other animated aquatics. Mrs. Puff claps, believing it's a good-humored joke. But everyone else in the class, except for overly friendly you-know-who, gets the hint and stays clear of the huge Flats, who like a real-life flounder is actually flat, with his eyes coming nearly to a point at the tip of his face.

"Hi, I'm SpongeBob," says our singular greeter after the newcomer takes the seat beside him.

"Hi, SpongeBob, I'm going to kick your butt," says Flats, invading the laughing SpongeBob's personal space and adding, "No, I mean it."

Freaked out to the umpteenth degree, SpongeBob raises his hand and asks Mrs. Puff, "May I be excused for the rest of my life?"

Our protagonist starts writing his last will and testament. Of course, he's leaving Gary's water dish to Gary. Who else would want it? SpongeBob even answers the phone saying, "Death row, next in line." It's Patrick on the other end, and SpongeBob comes up with the idea of using him for protection. Only Patrick is actually hanging out with Flats at the moment he calls. Seems they're old community college classmates. *Patrick went to college?*

SpongeBob finally approaches Mrs. Puff about concerns for his safety. He confides in her with the caveat, "Only if you promise to keep it between us." Naturally, Mrs. Puff comes back to him later in the day and says, "I talked to Flats for you. I used your name. . . . Flats is from a town where kicking someone's butt means that he wants to be your friend and maybe play some sports with you on weekends." Meanwhile, during Mrs. Puff's speech, Flats is in the background pounding a sand sculpture of SpongeBob, who later meets Flats's father only to find out that he too is afraid of his son.

"I gotta skip town. Start a new life. Live under an assumed name— BobPants SpongeSquare," says a frantic SpongeBob.

Even when Flats has an accident and SpongeBob saves his life by performing five straight hours of CPR (just to be certain, despite the medical attendants believing three minutes was enough), the bully still wants to kick his butt.

Then comes the moment of truth, when Flats kicks down the pineapple's front door to confront SpongeBob alone. SpongeBob closes his eyes to the pain he knows is coming. But Flats's blows comically have absolutely no effect on our porous protagonist.

"That tickles. . . . I'm absorbing his blows like I was made of some sort of spongy material," says a relieved SpongeBob.

Flats continues throwing blows at the sponge for an extended period of time until they're actually back in boating class, where Flats finally exhausts himself and falls to the floor with SpongeBob standing over him.

That when Mrs. Puff enters the classroom and ironically shouts, "SpongeBob, I can't believe you beat up a new student. I'm going to kick your butt!"

HURTFUL HUMOR

Recognizing the stand-up comedy craze of the 1980s and 1990s, during which Tom Kenny made his stand-up debut, the Krusty Krab (now the Komedy Krab) holds a comedy night with Mr. Krabs as emcee, wearing a Steve Martin–like faux arrow through his head.

SpongeBob takes the stage, greeting the crowd as "ladies and jelly-fish." There's nothing but the sound of crickets in response to his not-so-amusing observations about working in a fast-food restaurant. Then the hecklers begin to badger him.

Desperate for a witty observation, SpongeBob's gaze lands on Sandy sitting in the crowd. "Did you ever notice how big squirrels' teeth are?" he asks, getting a positive reaction from the crowd. "Hey, you could land a plane on those things." That snowballs into a barrage of squirrel jokes, with both the crowd and SpongeBob loving it. Only Sandy, who approaches SpongeBob after the show, is bothered by the comments.

"Those jokes are hurtful and you know it," says Sandy.

"I was just joking. . . . We've all got to laugh at ourselves once in a while," counters SpongeBob, temporarily putting Sandy at ease.

But the following day in a Bikini Bottom supermarket, strangers feel like it is okay to verbally abuse her, referencing the squirrel jokes they heard the previous night.

"Don't stand too close to the squirrel, Billy," a mother fish warns her child. "You'll catch its stupid."

So Sandy approaches SpongeBob backstage before his next stand-up performance.

"Since you've been telling them jokes, people have been treating me different," Sandy informs him.

SpongeBob really *hears* her this time. Unfortunately, he has no other jokes and starts to bomb on stage again.

"Tell the one about the squirrel and the light bulbs," screams Patrick from the packed audience.

SpongeBob realizes he has a choice to make: his friend or his stand-up career. He momentarily chooses his career, launching into more depre-cating squirrel humor.

After the show's conclusion, Sandy invites SpongeBob to her treedome and portrays every stereotype he's ascribed to her until he realizes that none of them are actually true.

Next time onstage, SpongeBob has a new routine.

"The only thing dumber than a squirrel is a sponge," says SpongeBob before widening the circle of his barbs. "Crabs are so cheap they can't even pay attention. . . . Now let me tell you about those fish. Boy, are they smelly. How can a creature who spends so much time in the water smell so bad?"

The crowd is wild with applause, as SpongeBob leads the way to them all laughing at themselves and not just at Sandy.

The episode perfectly fades out with a thumbs-up from Sandy as SpongeBob tells the audience, "And don't even get me started on starfish."

QUIZ QUESTION 13

Here's another two-part quiz. This one concerns SpongeBob's appearance. (1) How many holes are on the front facade of our porous protagonist? (2) What are the colors of the two stripes on SpongeBob's white tube socks? (Yes, they are always the same.)

The answer can be found after the book's conclusion.

I-M-A-G-I-N-A-T-I-O-N

Action!

Ever feel like you've got what it takes to be a great animator and storyteller? Want to know what it was like to walk in Stephen Hillenburg's shoes and create plots for *SpongeBob SquarePants*? Well, lots of fans have done exactly that. They've used two-inch action figures from the series and created their own stories by a process referred to as stop-motion. That's a cinematic technique in which a camera is repeatedly started and stopped, producing singular photos that are viewed in rapid succession, giving stationary figures the appearance of movement. There are apps that enable you to achieve this technique on your smartphone. Many fans of the series have done this, and you can view their episodes on You-Tube. Some newbies even added bubbles rising upward on the screen to give their work that authentic series look.

FAN FORUM

"To me, SpongeBob is the kind of show everyone has seen. I think I have seen almost every episode, as have many of my friends and class-mates. I love how the art style is as if a kid drew it. And I love how a lot of the facts on the show are true, as the show's creator was actually a marine biologist."—M. W.

14

GARY

SHELL OF A SURPRISE

Sometimes a side character catches the audience's fancy and becomes a bigger focus to the evolving plotlines than anyone ever intended. Plankton is a prime example of that (he'd be thrilled to hear his name associated with the word "bigger"). The same can be said about Gary, SpongeBob's pet sea snail, who was originally conceived by Stephen Hillenburg as nothing more than an animated piece of furniture in the pineapple—one that meows like a cat. However, a particular pair of first-season episodes, both relating to Gary's literary side, really sparked viewer interest in the evolving character, who is also voiced by Tom Kenny.

In "Culture Shock" (season 1, episode 10), Gary comes out of his shell (figuratively) and performs before a large audience at the Krusty Krab's talent show. Perched on a high stool with a microphone in front of him, Gary clears his throat in what sounds like a deep human voice. He then begins to meow poetry that he's written. In the audience, Sandy gushes and says, "He has such a way with words." Squidward even snidely refers to the snail as "Ginsberg," alluding to American poet Allen

Ginsberg, who was part of the Beat generation of the 1960s, along with writers such as Jack Kerouac and William S. Burroughs.

That literary connection becomes even more defined in "Sleepy Time" (season 1, episode 15), when SpongeBob is able to step inside the dreams of others, including Gary.

"In dreams, one is not tethered by earthly limitations," Gary responds to SpongeBob's amazement that he can speak in the dreamscape.

Gary no longer slithers but rather floats across the floor with his shell atop a closed Dr. Strange–like cape. Does he have a body beneath the fabric? We can only wonder.

The snail now towers over SpongeBob physically and mentally, as he inhabits a vast library of books. "Let me not mar that perfect dream," says Gary, quoting poet Emily Dickinson. But for the bewildered SpongeBob, Gary subsequently dumbs it down for him with a limerick about an old man from Nantucket.

NOT THE BOSS OF ME

Young kids who wish that they could make the rules in their households instead of their parents can both empathize with Gary's dilemmas and celebrate his victories. In "Gary Takes a Bath" (season 2, episode 13)—something the snail absolutely doesn't want to do—Gary meows, "You're not the boss of me." His owner can decipher it, but we can't. SpongeBob retorts the universal parental sentiment that every kid has heard: "It may be a free country, but you live in my house under my rules."

After Gary escapes the pineapple in order to avoid bathing, he appears to have climbed a tall tree (something cats occasionally do). SpongeBob grabs a ladder to retrieve him. But once the snail's owner steps onto the top branches, he discovers that the meowing he heard is just a recording on a phonograph disguised to look like the snail. Gary is actually on the ground. He removes the ladder, stranding SpongeBob in the tree, who eventually falls into a huge mud puddle below, consequently needing a bath himself. Dirty trick, but cleverly funny.

I-M-A-GI-N-A-T-I-O-N

To entice Gary into a taking a bath, SpongeBob paints the tub to look like a pirate's treasure chest. He even pulls two bars of soap from the tub and calls them gold doubloons. But Gary isn't having any part of this fantasy play. So SpongeBob picks up the phone and places an imaginary call to a fancy French restaurant, pretending to inform the establishment, which probably serves escargot (snails) on its menu, "I've got a nasty snail here who won't take a bath." Ah, creative pet training.

DOG OR CAT?

Are the pet snails of Bikini Bottom—and there are plenty of them—more like cats or dogs? The answer is undoubtedly both, spurred by whichever connection momentarily serves the writers' interests best. Sure, Gary meows, occasionally purrs like a feline, and doesn't want a bath. But SpongeBob takes him to the Bikini Bottom Snail Park, which resembles a typical dog park, where Gary can run and ramble (okay, at a snail's pace) with his friends. And how does he get there? SpongeBob walks him through the streets on a leash.

In the sixth season's "Grooming Gary" (episode 9), SpongeBob becomes intent on Gary winning a medal at the local pet show. The show's sponsor is the Bikini Bottom Kennel Club, a takeoff on the famed Westminster Kennel Club, which is dedicated to the sport of dogs. Incidentally, that episode is when mild-mannered Gary goes Braveheart, leading a snail revolution against a league of self-absorbed owners who excessively primp and embarrass their pets in order to possess an award.

PET LIFE

Gary sleeps on a thin pile of newspapers spread out next to his food dish, which displays his name. Water dish? Don't be silly; he lives in the sea. Like most gastropods, Gary leaves a trail of slime behind him as he moves. While tracking down his missing pet, SpongeBob once identified Gary's slime trail by tasting it. Gross! The pineapple's main hatch/doorway sometimes has a smaller built-in door, resembling our doggy doors, so that Gary can come and go as he pleases. Gary does his personal business in an indoor sandbox hidden out of the way. It apparently reeks because SpongeBob approaches it with a clothespin on his nose. As for food, SpongeBob prepares his pet seaweed noodle stew, a thick green slop. But when his owner is too busy to cook for him, Gary either chows down on store-bought bagged food or canned Snail-Po, inspired by our pets' Alpo brand food.

"I've been feeding this to Gary for years and I don't even know what it tastes like," ponders SpongeBob while studying an open can of Snail-Po. So the owner slips his tongue inside. "*Blaaah!*" His taste buds are so repulsed that a member of the sales team at Snail-Po World Headquarters actually feels a "disturbance" in ocean tides.

QUIZ QUESTION 14

Here's a colorful two-part quiz concerning Gary. One question is easy and the other more difficult. (1) What trio of colors comprise Gary's shell? (2) For hardcore fans: believe it or not, Gary wears a pair of shoes beneath his unsegmented body. What color are they? Here's a hint: They're two-toned.

The answer can be found after the book's conclusion.

RELATIONSHIP GARY

Gary's been bitten by the love bug on multiple occasions. He had a crush on a female snail from the snail park named Mary after the pair shared the teeter-totter together. But that romance didn't have a shell of a chance of working out after Mary caught sight of her former flame. Then there was Squidward's $1,700 pedigreed snail named Snellie, who arrived via special delivery from a breeder. Are there snail mills in Bikini Bottom? Obviously, the snooty Squidward, who refers to Gary as a "mutt," won't allow such a union. Perhaps Gary held a grudge about that, because in the eleventh season's "Chatterbox Gary" (episode 10), our favorite gastropod is given a device that allows him to speak English. Squidward is impressed by Gary's vocabulary and can't wait to show the snail his paintings and other artistic works. But Gary almost gleefully refers to them as "unsophisticated" and "tacky." It is in that episode that Gary shows incredible love for his owner, despite their many battles, by calling him "PapaBob."

ONE OF A KIND

A snail with legs? That's right. In "Gary's Got Legs" (season 12, episode 4), SpongeBob goes Doctor Moreau (the protagonist who combines species in the 1896 sci-fi classic novel *The Island of Doctor Moreau* by H. G. Wells) on us by giving Gary a pair of his own legs, striped tube socks and shoes included.

Don't worry. The pair that SpongeBob gives away instantly grow back. Many creatures can regenerate limbs, but obviously not that quickly. Starfish are amazing at it, and so are sponges, who can completely regenerate themselves from just a fragment of their body or even a single cell.

How does being the only snail with legs affect Gary? He completely takes over the snail park, becomes a Casanova with the female snails, and boots a bully worm and its owner into orbit with a swift kick. Later on, SpongeBob gives Gary a pair of his arms as well. When his owner is too sick to take his shift at the Krusty Krab, Gary fills in for him at the grill, slinging krabby patties. The customers rightly complain, however: "Too much slime on my patty!"

LOOKING BACK

PERSPECTIVE: TOM KENNY

Q: How did your overall journey and experiences contribute to your delivery and comic timing in doing voices?

TK: I didn't get my first voice-over work in cartoons until I was thirty. It took me several years of persistence before I was able to get my nose under that professional tent. I believe that timing comes from experience. I think that everything I did along the way, being a jack-of-all-trades—doing stand-up around the country, sketch comedy on TV in *The Edge* [an early 1990s series in which Kenny, his future wife Jill Talley, and actors such as Jennifer Aniston and Wayne Knight (Newman from *Seinfeld*) took part], and singing in a rock and roll band where I needed to quickly memorize songs—contributed to it. I had developed this oddball set of skills, as the Native Americans preach: *use every part of the buffalo*. Skill A enabled me to master skill B, and all of those things combined gave me a sense of timing.

CLASSIC LINES

Here are some classic *SpongeBob SquarePants* lines that illustrate the characters' personalities and thought processes so well. All are delivered with expert timing, increasing their impact.

"Life is like a bucket of wood shavings, except when it's in a pail. Then it's like a pail of wood shavings."—SpongeBob (Tom Kenny)

"Breathe on your own time. I don't pay you to breathe." —Mr. Krabs (Clancy Brown)

"Good morning, class. Sorry I'm late. I got caught in traffic on the way in here when that whole I'm-going-to-be-doing-this-for-the-rest-of-my-life thing reared its ugly head."—Mrs. Puff (Mary Jo Catlett)

"Stupidity isn't a virus. But it sure is spreading like one." —Sandy Cheeks (Carolyn Lawrence)

"Meow."—Gary (Tom Kenny)

"I can deny it no longer, I am small."—Plankton (Mr. Lawrence)

"I know a lot about head injuries. Believe me."—Patrick (Bill Fagerbakke)

"And now, ladies and gentlemen, the moment you've all been waiting for. We've saved the best for last. Put your hands together for the incomparable Squidward."—Squidward (Rodger Bumpass)

"We can do this the hard way or the easy way. Or the medium way. Or the semi-medium-easy-hard way. Or the sort-of-hard with a touch of awkward-easy-difficult-challenging way."— SpongeBob (Tom Kenny)

MERMAID MAN AND BARNACLE BOY

HERO WORSHIP

Over the first six seasons of *SpongeBob SquarePants*, undersea crime fighters Mermaid Man and Barnacle Boy were featured in a total of seven episodes. Like the dual feline/canine influence on Gary the snail, this aged superhero pair owe their creation to both Aquaman and Aqualad and the dynamic duo of Batman and Robin.

"Fleet and forceful, with the ability to assemble and charge the creatures of the deep, Mermaid Man and his young associate Barnacle Boy fight for all creatures that live in the sea against the forces of evil," states the announcer, as we watch a video montage of the pair in their youthful prime.

Of course, that was several decades ago. In a beautifully comedic twist, Mermaid Man and Barnacle Boy are now senior citizens and residents of Bikini Bottom's Shady Shoals Rest Home.

"Old people are the greatest," says SpongeBob, whose faith in their abilities continues. "They're full of wisdom and experience."

Batman often commands, "To the Bat Poles! To the Batmobile! To the Batcave!" However, Mermaid Man, who waits in line to eat at the

Shady Shoals cafeteria, shouts, "To the meatloaf! To the broccoli!" And when his back stiffens up, "To the chiropractor!"

The superheroes are voiced by acting and comedy legends Ernest Borgnine (Mermaid Man), who won the Academy Award for best actor in 1955, and Tim Conway (Barnacle Boy), a five-time Emmy Award winner. What's the ocean connection here? Borgnine and Conway starred together in a 1960s TV comedy titled *McHale's Navy*, which took place in the Pacific during World War II.

TOP FIVE EPISODE COUNTDOWN: NUMBER FOUR

My number-four episode in the countdown is the debut of the geriatric guardians of the deep in the premiere season's "Mermaid Man and Barnacle Boy" (episode 6).

SpongeBob and Patrick are playing superhero, dressed up as their idols Mermaid Man (SpongeBob) and Barnacle Boy (Patrick), using donuts around their fingers as super-powered rings. The pair sees Squidward sunbathing outside his house using a shiny reflector to intensify the sun's rays. They pretend that he's an archvillain named Reflecto. To rid himself of the annoying duo, Squidward tells them to go visit the real Mermaid Man and Barnacle Boy at the local retirement home.

Upon meeting their heroes at the Shady Shoals Rest Home, an awed SpongeBob and Patrick can't believe that Mermaid Man and Barancle Boy are on hiatus.

"You can't retire. There's evil afoot," says SpongeBob.

That word "evil" sends Mermaid Man into a frenzy—and a wrestling match with a water cooler, a battle he loses.

To rebuild their heroes' confidence, SpongeBob stages a fake robbery dressed as a damsel in distress, with Patrick disguised to look amazingly like the Hamburglar from the McDonald's ads. When that plan fails, they decide to help out by painting Mermaid Man and Barnacle Boy's legendary invisible boatmobile.

"Oh, it's supposed to be invisible!" rages Barnacle Boy, who then convinces his partner to come out of retirement so that they can put a stop to the antics of SpongeBob and Patrick.

The superheroes put on their power rings, recite the oath, and then begin to throw water-balls (just like Aquaman) at SpongeBob, much to his awestruck glee.

"Mumbling morays," says Barnacle Boy, emulating Robin's use of alliteration, "it's not working, Mermaid Man."

"He's absorbing it like some kind of evil sponge," adds Mermaid Man before the aged heroes decide to dog paddle in faster and faster circles around SpongeBob and Patrick, mimicking another famed technique that has stopped many villains.

An excited Patrick screams, "It's the raging whirlpool!"

"The fiends, they're actually enjoying it," says Mermaid Man.

"Do it again! Do it again!" chant SpongeBob and Patrick at the conclusion of the wild spin cycle.

Then Mermaid Man uses his telekinesis (à la Aquaman) to summon the creatures of the deep to his aid. But the only ones who show up are the residents of the rest home with their canes, walkers, and wheelchairs. But they have enough combined strength to toss SpongeBob and Patrick all the way back to the pineapple.

"Mission accomplished, Patrick," says SpongeBob, successful in restoring their heroes to their former luster—sort of.

"I feel five years younger!" exclaims a quasi-victorious Mermaid Man. "Oh, it's good to be back!"

WHY IT GETS HIGH MARKS

The conception of the two aged supers alone is amazing—a reflection of senior citizen Aquaman and Aqualad/Batman and Robin. But the interactions between young and old here really shine. It's innocent, hilarious, and masterfully voiced by Ernest Borgnine and Tim Conway. It was an absolute coup to get them both to appear, and the opportunity wasn't wasted.

QUIZ QUESTION 15

Do you recall the oath that Mermaid Man and Barnacle Boy recite when they touch rings?

The answer can be found after the book's conclusion.

NEW ADVENTURES

In "Mermaid Man and Barnacle Boy II" (season 1, episode 20), the reinvigoration of the aged heroes spawns an updated Saturday morning TV show titled *The New Adventures of Mermaid Man and Barnacle Boy*. That in turn inspires a new kids' breakfast cereal featuring the heroic pair on the box. The cereal is loaded with bran (to ensure your time on the bathroom's porcelain throne *passes* more easily). The prize in each cereal box? A pair of dentures.

SpongeBob enters and wins a tribute contest sponsored by the cereal company by constructing life-size statues of the heroes made of krabby patties. As the grand prize, he wins the conch shell, which instantly summons the heroes to battle evil. But SpongeBob begins blowing it for smaller problems: the annoyed heroes arrive to open a stuck mayonnaise jar, read SpongeBob a bedtime story, and unclog a drain.

Later, SpongeBob more than makes it up to Mermaid Man and Barnacle Boy by freeing them from imprisonment inside the evil Dirty Bubble. How? SpongeBob wants the Dirty Bubble's autograph and his sharpened pencil accidentally pops him, freeing his heroes.

COSTUMES, GADGETS, AND VILLAINS

Mermaid Man's costume closely resembles that of Aquaman. But let's not focus too hard on the pink bedroom slippers he currently wears. He has an orange top, green gloves, and a belt buckle with the letter *M*, as opposed to Aquaman's *A* belt buckle. Like Batman, Mermaid Man's belt serves as a utility belt with plenty of gadgets. One of those gadgets is a shrink ray. SpongeBob gets his hands on the belt when Mermaid Man leaves it behind after visiting the Krusty Krab. Naturally, SpongeBob can't control his excitement of having the belt and accidentally shrinks nearly the entire population of Bikini Bottom.

Patrick suggests that SpongeBob simply flip the belt buckle upside down (as a form of going in reverse), turning the *M* on the belt into a *W*.

"You know what the problem is? You have it set to '*M*' for mini. When it should be set to '*W*' for "wambo," says Patrick, spinning the letter around.

"I don't think *wambo* is a real word," says SpongeBob.

"Come on. You know. I wambo. You wambo. He, she, me wambo. Wambo. Wamboing . . . wombology—the study of wambo. It's first grade, SpongeBob," says Patrick.

Of course, that idea doesn't work, so SpongeBob comes up with the solution of shrinking the rest of the town, structures and all. He does it, and everything seems perfect at that point. That's when Hillenburg and the writing staff throw the perfect curve. It seems that Plankton has been out of town visiting during this shrinking debacle. Wonderfully, he returns at the end of the episode as a giant. Hooray for Plankton!

NOT-SO-EVIL DOERS

Who are the undersea villains? This salty rogues' gallery includes Sinister Slug, Atomic Flounder, the Dreaded Jumbo Shrimp (which is an oxymoron, a contradictory figure of speech), the Dirty Bubble, and Man Ray— inspired by Aquaman's Black Manta. But what if more than one archvillain strikes at any time? Then we'd need a bigger superhero team. Stephen Hillenburg and the writers borrowed from DC Comics' Justice League by creating IJLSA, an acronym for International Justice League of Super Acquaintances. It features SpongeBob as the Quickster, Squidward as

Captain Magma (that's appropriate because he enjoys blowing his top like a volcano), Patrick as the Elastic Waistband (who's tubby?), and Sandy as Miss Appear, who can turn invisible. The criminals have a team too. Its sour acronym is EVIL—Every Villain Is Lemons.

TENURE TENSIONS

Have Mermaid Man and Barnacle Boy developed any personal friction over their long tenure together? Well, there is one particular point of contention on Barnacle Boy's part. The sixty-eight-year-old superhero now wants to be called "Barnacle Man." Things comes to a head when Mermaid Man insists on ordering a kids' meal for Barnacle Boy at the Krusty Krab.

"I don't want a pipsqueak patty. I want an adult-size krabby patty. . . . Don't you see what you're doing? You're treating me like a child," insists Barnacle Boy.

Then Squidward, ever the instigator, offers him a bib and a high chair. It leads to a great storyline in "Mermaid Man and Barnacle Boy V" (season 3, episode 12), as Barnacle Boy (uh, Barnacle *Man*) crosses over to the dark side and becomes a villain for a while before the heroic pair eventually reunite. Incidentally, Barnacle Boy doesn't have too far to go to reach the shadowy dark side, since Mr. Krabs is too cheap to light the whole restaurant.

16

THE KRUSTY KRAB

LET'S EAT

A good portion of the *SpongeBob SquarePants* series takes place inside the Krusty Krab, Bikini Bottom's most successful fast-food dine-in/carry-out restaurant. Its physical design is actually based on a standard lobster trap with its arched sides displaying a netted window design.

Psst. Don't tell Larry the Lobster.

"The Krusty Krab. Come spend your money here!" states the establishment's first commercial.

The signature item there is the krabby patty. "It's only the most mouth-watering, appetizing food in the seven seas," states Mr. Krabs.

The reason for the eatery's success? Some say it rests upon a young sponge's ability to wield a spatula as a fry cook and nestle a blanket of cheese over a patty. Others might believe it's Eugene Krabs's secret krabby patty formula or his frugal economics. Few believe it's customer service, since Squidward runs the register. Whatever the hypothetical answer, Stephen Hillenburg's culinary cartoon creation has more recognition and gravitas in our culture today than many real-life fast-food franchises.

Lobster traps like these were the model for the Krusty Krab. Can you see the resemblance?
Getty/Kirkikis

Do you know of another establishment that sponsors double-patty midnight madness? Here's how Hillenburg originally described it in his pitch bible: "This is the Crusty Crab, a local fast food joint serving up the popular fare of barnacle burgers, coral fries and salty shakes. Once you walk in the door you'll be treated to the friendliest customer service this side of the continental shelf. That is if Sponge Boy happens to be working that day, which is most likely the case because he hardly ever takes a day off. Never have the words, 'My pleasure to serve you,' been taken to such extremes. Enjoy your lunch!"

Ever wonder what you might order if you had the opportunity to eat at the Krusty Krab? Well, throughout the series' many seasons we've had multiple looks at the menu board: Galley Grub. "Galley" is a term used for a ship's kitchen. Most times the writing below the menu's title is merely out-of-focus scribbles, but every now and then we get a good look at exactly what's available.

We'll concentrate on just a pair of scenes where the menu is clearly legible so we can compare and contrast. In the premiere season's "Pickles" (season 1, episode 6), where Bubble Bass tries to ruin SpongeBob's reputation and confidence as a fry cook by twice claiming the pickles are missing from his patty, we're presented with the menu in full. Its main fare consists of the Krabby Patty, Krabby Combo, and Krabby Deluxe. The choice of sides are Seaweed Salad (for more health-conscious consumers) and Coral Bits, which sound like they should be very crunchy.

What's the process for building a krabby patty? "First bun, then patty, followed ketchup, mustard, pickles . . . onions, lettuce, cheese, tomato, and bun," confirms SpongeBob.

By the third season's "Mermaid Man and Barnacle Boy V" (episode 12), there have been plenty of additions to the menu. There are Kelp Rings and Golden Loaf (perhaps onion based?), both of which you can get with sauce for an extra charge. Now that's the Mr. Krabs we know. Sailors Surprise is also listed. What is it? Your guess is as good as anyone's. Finally, beverages make their debut appearance in print—Seafoam Soda and Kelp Shake. This episode also lets us know that kids can order a Silly Meal with a toy, obviously inspired by the McDonald's Happy Meal.

Regular customers can get incredibly creative with their orders, especially when SpongeBob has that flattop grill humming. Maybe you'd like a king-size Ultra Krabby Supreme with the works (double battered and fried on a stick), or a Triple Krabby Supreme on a kelp bun with extra sea pickles. Don't be shy about asking.

Here are some additional menu listings we've seen over the course of the series, which the writing staff obviously had a very good time with:

Double Krabby Patty
Krabby Junior-Junior
Jumbo Small Patty
Junior, Senior, Sophomore Patty
Quarter Ouncer Double Pounder

Super Double Triple Patty
Jumbo Patty Super Jumbo
Captain Olaf's Special
Super Seaweed Shake

Pop star Katy Perry once dressed as a krabby patty for a costume gala at New York City's Metropolitan Museum of Art. Her head rose above the sesame seed bun, with lettuce, tomato, melted cheese, and a pair of patties circling her midsection.

In the sweets aisle, several different companies have at one time or another produced gummy candies both shaped like and named for the krabby patty.

OTHER OPTIONS FOR BOTTOMITES

Where else can diners in Bikini Bottom go for a bite to eat besides the Krusty Krab? We wouldn't recommend the Chum Bucket because the reviews are terrible, especially for the chumbalaya, a takeoff on the Louisiana-born dish jambalaya. Not to mention the fact that Plankton might attempt to either brainwash you or remove your brain completely. Obviously, it's an establishment that favors blind allegiance by its customers. But there is Weeny Hut and Weeny Hut Jr.'s serving weenies (both on buns for consumption and as customers) as well as ice cream, donuts, tacos, and pizza (Pizza Castle). For residents who'd rather fix a quick snack at home, there's always a sea-nut butter and jellyfish jam sandwich.

PASSING FADS

Even bottom-feeders feel the need for new taste sensations. The stubborn ears of Mr. Krabs hear this loud and clear when an uninspired customer arrives at the door of the Krusty Krab in "Patty Hype" (season 2, episode 5). "Where's the pizazz?" inquires the hungry aquatic with no desire for a traditional krabby patty. "Look at this place. What's the theme here, 'underwater'? Boring!" To make matters worse, Mr. Krabs's regular customers are flocking to a new restaurant called Shell City, which features a talking dog that eventually learns to sing. That's when SpongeBob presents Mr. Krabs with his newest creation—pretty patties, which come in six colors: green, red, purple, orange, pink, and yellow.

Krabs scoffs at the idea, belittling SpongeBob, who sets up a roadside stand. Pretty patties quickly become a megahit, and everyone waits in line to buy one.

"Line? I never had a line," pouts Mr. Krabs.

The stand makes such an enormous profit that SpongeBob and Patrick shred, burn, and give the overflow cash back to their customers—blasphemy in Mr. Krabs's eyes.

A jealous Mr. Krabs then trades SpongeBob the key to his restaurant in exchange for the stand, demonstrating both SpongeBob's limitless affection for the Krusty Krab and Mr. Krabs's passion for money.

The next morning, though, Hillenburg and the writers give Krabs his just desserts. Pretty patties have a startling effect on residents, turning them different colors to their absolute dismay and threats of lawsuits.

It's a colorful end to another of Mr. Krabs's money-grubbing schemes.

In "Jellyfish Hunters" (season 2, episode 19), SpongeBob shares his jellyfish jelly with the customers, who begin putting it on their krabby patties. The result is *wow!*

"Here, Mr. Krabs. Take your taste buds on a journey," says SpongeBob, handing his boss a jelly-loaded patty.

"Messing with the patty's formula. That's mutiny" is Mr. Krabs's initial reaction.

That's when a customer with a jellied patty approaches Mr. Krabs and says, "Sir, this is the greatest thing I've ever eaten. I'm going to come back here for lunch every day for the rest of my life."

Almost instantaneously, Mr. Krabs sees dollar signs.

Mr. Krabs, however, goes overboard by trying corner the jellyfish market and capturing the entire population of Jellyfish Fields. Naturally, they get loose from a giant container via Mr. Krabs's own bad karma. "The door is voice-activated and will only open if I say, 'Open,'" he says, realizing his unfortunate choice of a word, before all the jellyfish escape and zap him.

"I'm taking jelly off the menu," affirms a crisply toasted Mr. Krabs.

BENEATH THE SURFACE

Stephen Hillenburg and the writers make an important statement about nature's delicate balance, especially in the face of profiteers. The subtle message in "Jellyfish Hunters" is totally spot-on without being preachy and reflects the conflict between nature and humankind both on land and in the seas.

THE LAST HOLDOUT

One Bikini Bottom aquatic claims he never tasted a krabby patty.

"That's me," says Squidward. "Never have. Never will."

"Those words. Is it possible to use them in a sentence like that?" responds a shocked and amazed SpongeBob, who makes it a priority to tempt his coworker into just one tiny bite.

Of course, Squidward reluctantly does and gets secretly hooked on the circular fast-food fare, and steaming patties fill his dizzying and disjointed nightmarish dreams. So Squidward raids the Krusty Krab in the early morning hours. SpongeBob finds him there but not before Squidward had scarfed down enough patties to explode from the inside out.

"I remember my first krabby patty," mocks the ambulance attendant, transporting Squidward's bodiless but alert head to the hospital.

QUIZ QUESTION 16

SpongeBob finds Squidward sneaking a krabby patty at the Krusty Krab at 3:00 a.m. Why was SpongeBob there? What obsessive chore does our porous protagonist perform at that exact time every morning?

The answer can be found after the book's conclusion.

FAUX FAMOUS

Like the Krusty Krab, other fictitious eateries have made an impact on our collective consciousness. They include Arnold's Drive-In from the TV series *Happy Days*, Bob's Burgers from the animated series *Bob's Burgers*, the village of Hogsmeade's Three Broomsticks from *Harry Potter*, Central Perk in the TV series *Friends*, and Monk's Café in *Seinfeld*. *Bon appétit.*

If you're in Madison, Wisconsin, on Halloween, check out a restaurant called Bierock, if you can recognize it. For the past several years, the establishment transforms itself into something different on October 31. In previous years, it has become Moe's Tavern from *The Simpsons* and the cantina from *Star Wars*. In 2020, though, Bierock became the Krusty Krab. It served krabby patties, sea dogs, kelp slaw, and barnacle crisps. Due to COVID-19 restrictions, there was no indoor dining, but all of the take-out fare was delivered to waiting cars by staff dressed like the characters from the *SpongeBob SquarePants* series.

Now that's getting into the proper Halloween spirit!

17

MUSIC, BROADWAY, MOVIES, AND BAND GEEKS

THE MUSIC LIBRARY

Music has been amazingly meaningful in the *SpongeBob SquarePants* series, from the opening strains of its theme song—"Oooooh, who lives in a pineapple under the sea?"—to the Hawaiian background music and silly songs that punctuate the plots.

For example, the song "Loop de Loop" helps SpongeBob overcome the fact that he's forgotten how to tie his shoes, which is logical, since the episode "Your Shoe's Untied" (season 2, episode 1) suggests that they had been tied since he was an embryo. "The Campfire Song Song" (that's right, say "song" twice), with its energetic and superfun "C-A-M-P-F-I-R-E S-O-N-G song" lyric from "The Camping Episode" (season 3, episode 17), is now sung at real-life summer camps around the country.

Sandy expresses her homesickness through the melancholy of "Texas Song," bringing SpongeBob and Patrick to tears about a place they've never even been. Then there's the first film's "The Goofy Goober Song," the kiddie sing-along theme of a mascot peanut (sea-nut) in a total spoof of Chuck E. Cheese.

Creator Stephen Hillenburg thought it was essential for the series to develop its own music library, and he was absolutely spot-on. *What are your favorite* SpongeBob-*related songs?*

There have been several faux cartoon bands on the series as well. They include Ned and the Needlefish, Boys Who Cry (a favorite boy band of Pearl Krabs, which played at her sixteenth birthday party), and Sting Ray 5000. Among the real-life artists featured beneath the animated waves are Pink, Davy Jones of the Monkees (misspelled just as the Beatles did to emphasize the musical term *beat*), David Bowie, Tiny Tim, Gene Simmons, Biz Markie, Dee Snider, Victoria Beckham, and the heavy metal band Pantera. And let's not forget that Tom Kenny performs in a real-life rock band aptly named Tom Kenny and the High Seas.

OPENING NIGHT

SpongeBob SquarePants: The Broadway Musical debuted on Broadway at the Palace Theater in 2017. The plot? Bikini Bottom is threatened by a volcano called Mount Humongous. Sandy invents a way to save the underwater city. However, the aquatics, not completely trusting a surface animal, debate whether her science actually might be the cause of their impending troubles. It's a story about trust and friendship, with Sponge-Bob trying to bridge the gap between his friends and save the day. Will hot magma or beautifully iridescent soap bubbles shower down on the community at the final curtain?

The musical is filled with spectacular songs such as "BFF," written by Plain White T's for SpongeBob and Patrick; "(I Guess I) Miss You," written by John Legend; and "Bikini Bottom Boogie," penned by Steven Tyler and Joe Perry of Aerosmith, who also double as an undersea band called the Electric Skates.

TWO MORE FEATURE FILMS

More than a decade after the first film, *The SpongeBob SquarePants Movie* (2004), *The SpongeBob Movie: Sponge out of Water* (2015) splashed onto the big screen. The magic of CGI (computer-generated imagery) brings the Bikini Bottom crew to life in the real world. Well, that and a magical book with the ability to turn text on the written page into reality. With the help of a powerful bottlenose dolphin named Bubbles, who gives the undersea characters the ability to breathe air and follow the smell of the stolen krabby patty secret formula, they set out to save their underwater community, which has become a ravenous wasteland without the presence of the delectable patties. It seems Mr. Krabs can't remember his own formula.

I know what you're thinking: Plankton stole the formula. Hold tight to your sea-salted popcorn, because Plankton is actually on the side of right in this movie. SpongeBob even tries to teach him the word "teamwork," but despite Plankton's revelation toward good, it comes out of his tiny mouth as "time bomb."

Along with SpongeBob, Patrick, Squidward, Sandy, and Mr. Krabs, Plankton transforms into a superhero as the squad battles the pirate Burger Beard. That's right, *Burger* Beard (played by actor Antonia Banderas), who has purloined the secret krabby patty formula.

The heroic Plankton resembles the Incredible Hulk. SpongeBob becomes Invincibubble, with a bubble wand protruding from the top of his porous head—brilliant! Sandy is the Rodent, a real-life squirrel. Mr. Krabs turns into the robotic Sir Pinch-a-Lot to highlight his claws, and Squidward becomes Sour Note, reflecting his off-key musical abilities.

The film is dedicated to Ernest Borgnine, the voice of Mermaid Man, who passed away in 2012. Actor Tim Conway, the longtime voice of Barnacle Boy, voiced a seagull for the film in his final animated role before his death in 2019.

Rest in peace, Mermaid Man and Barnacle Boy.

SpongeBob and his friends in 3D. What a beach day this could be. *Paramount/Photofest*
© *Paramount Pictures*

The SpongeBob Movie: Sponge on the Run (2020) is the first film re-
leased after the untimely passing of creator Stephen Hillenburg in 2018.
Gary is snail-napped by a vain King Poseidon, who uses snail slime to
eradicate facial wrinkles.

In *Wizard of Oz*–like fashion, SpongeBob and Patrick are given a fake
talisman or charm in the form of a "challenge coin" by a tumbling sea sage
(played by Keanu Reeves), which convinces the pair that they have the
needed courage to rescue Gary from Poseidon's Atlantic City domain.
The film also introduces alternative storylines concerning how the essential Bikini Bottom characters first met in their younger years at Camp
Coral, including SpongeBob's adoption of Gary.

Eventually, SpongeBob's own courage (without the coin) and friendship have a profound influence on the friendless Poseidon, monumen-
tally changing his life for the better. It's amazing how the innocence and
loyalty of SpongeBob have the ability to make an impression on powerful
characters. And why not? The spongy yellow fry cook who wants nothing
more than to be our friend seems to make us all heed our better angels.

PIRATE ROLL CALL

In the second *SpongeBob SquarePants*–inspired film, the audience meets Burger Beard, a pirate and real-life purveyor of fast food on land, who uses his boatmobile as a ship-shaped food truck to build a burger empire with the stolen krabby patty formula.

But what's a zany nautical world without a host of buccaneers and swashbucklers with which to contend?

Our continuing roll call of pirates in the series begins with the real-life Patchy the Pirate, played by Tom Kenny. His parrot sidekick is no clichéd "Polly"; instead, Patchy's parrot is named Potty (voiced by Stephen Hillenburg). That's an example of toilet humor at its best by the writing staff.

Next is Painty the Pirate, who lives within the borders of a framed portrait and kicks off the show's theme song at the start of practically every episode.

Then there's the Flying Dutchman, a ghostly animated antagonist based on the centuries-old Dutch legend of a ship with a ghost crew doomed to sail the seas forever, never making port. In the series, he has some obvious problems relating to others. Like any pirate, he's protective of his buried treasure. And on Halloween night, this version of the Flying Dutchman, resentful of anyone who dares to dress up like him, makes the rounds in Bikini Bottom stealing souls.

In pirate parlance, the term "shanghai" means forcibly making someone join the crew on your ship, a kind of sea-kidnapping. In the episode "Shanghaied" (season 2, episode 13), the Flying Dutchman shanghais SpongeBob, Patrick, and Squidward before the Dutchman realizes he's a whole lot scarier without this trio as his crew. How did the residents of Conch Street encounter the pirate? SpongeBob was eating breakfast, looking for his prize in the Kelpo cereal box, when a huge anchor on a rope fell from above through his pineapple. His response was to run to Squidward's house screaming, "The sky had a baby from my cereal box!" Hysterically, Patrick had the exact same reaction. So how much do these two know about biology?

What about those pirate eye patches?

Painty has one over his left eye. Tom Kenny really can't seem to remember whether Patchy's eye patch goes over the left or right eye, because it changes several times. Neither the Flying Dutchman nor Burger Beard wear an eye patch. But Patrick, when he dresses as Blind Beard, makes up for that by wearing a patch over both eyes and stumbling around blindly. Please don't let him fall overboard. What am I saying? He lives underwater!

In "Arrgh" (season 1, episode 17), with Mr. Krabs as their captain, SpongeBob and Patrick become not-so-serious pirates after playing the Flying Dutchman's Treasure Hunt board game. It's where Mr. Krabs teaches them to say "arrgh" instead of "okey-dokey." The word "arrgh" is an exclamation supposedly used by pirates and other seafarers to voice disgust.

TOP FIVE EPISODE COUNTDOWN: NUMBER THREE

Our number-three episode in the countdown is a music-themed triumph of animated storytelling and laughter titled "Band Geeks" (season 2, episode 15). Apparently, Stephen Hillenburg is happy to glorify the halftime marching band over the football team, even on the world's biggest primetime stage, the Super Bowl—excuse me, the Bubble Bowl.

Here's how the hilarious fun unfolds: the sound of Squidward practicing the clarinet echoes through Bikini Bottom when his doorbell rings. The aquatic holding a medical bag says to Squidward, "We're with the pet hospital down the street and I understand you have a dying animal on the premises." Ouch!

Squidward then gets a shell-phone call from his old band-class rival, Squilliam, whose band can't make its scheduled appearance at the following week's Bubble Bowl. Unable to tell the snooty Squilliam the truth, that he has no band, Squidward accepts and puts up posters that read: "Looking to add fulfillment to your dull, dull life? Then become part of the greatest musical sensation to ever hit Bikini Bottom and be adored by thousands of people you don't know." Did Squidward really say *people* and not fish or other sea life? Stay tuned. That becomes important.

Most of Bikini Bottom shows up for band practice, with Squidward acting as the maestro. "How many of you have played musical instruments before?" he asks. Plankton wants to know if instruments of torture count.

"Is mayonnaise an instrument?" asks Patrick Star. Squidward tells him no, anticipating his follow-up question. "Horseradish is not an instrument either," he says, as a disappointed Patrick lowers his hand.

After four days of horrifically comical practice, Squidward's only hope is to instruct his musicians to play loudly and hope that no one in the audience will notice their deficiencies. But SpongeBob rallies the band together upon Squidward's departure, asking them who'd come to their rescue in the past. The answers: firefighters and ambulance workers. "If we all could just pretend Squidward was a fireman or some guy in an ambulance, then I'm sure we can all pull together and discover what it truly means to be in a marching band," says SpongeBob.

"Yeah, for the fireman!" screams a fish in the background before the band resumes practicing on their own.

The night of the Bubble Bowl, Squilliam is in attendance. He's there to belittle Squidward. "I just wanted to watch you blow it," smirks Squilliam. That is, until SpongeBob and the band arrives, actually marching in step. With the entire band on the riser, they're elevated up to the playing field of the Bubble Bowl, where the stands are packed with actual *people*.

"These are some ugly-looking fish," says Patrick.

"Maybe we're near one of those toxic waste dumps," says Sponge-Bob, with the crowd going wild.

A hesitant Squidward gives the band their cue, and the surprising result is magic.

SpongeBob launches into the vocals for "Sweet Victory," a pulsing rock standard written by Bob Kulick and performed by David Glen Eisley. With Patrick on electric drums and a guitar solo by Mrs. Puff, the band positively captivates the crowd.

The performance causes Squilliam to faint, and the final shot is a freeze-frame of Squidward jumping high into the air to celebrate his band's musical victory.

Applause.

WHY IT GETS HIGH MARKS

"Band Geeks" is simply an outstanding mix of animation and live action, filled with drama, emotion, and most of all, music. It's great to see the cast come together on an endeavor with as many moving parts as a band. And who doesn't want to see Squidward succeed on a musical stage thanks to his friends?

QUIZ QUESTION 17

Who was the first recording artist to have a song on the *SpongeBob SquarePants* series? Hint: It occurred in the very first episode.

The answer can be found after the book's conclusion.

FAN FORUM

"Growing up, SpongeBob SquarePants was my hero. Most little kids call their parents or grandparents their hero, but my hero was a yellow talking sponge. I remember being glued to the television before and after school, waiting to see that goofy sponge come across the screen. *SpongeBob SquarePants* will forever be remembered as being the foundation of my childhood."—K. A.

PERSPECTIVE: TOM KENNY

Q: How do you feel knowing what the characters have meant to people of so many ages?

TK: I'm really proud of what we've achieved with the *SpongeBob SquarePants* series, proud of the entire team, or what I like to call "The Whole Sponge." I have friendships within the cast, and it's been a quarter of a century that we've been together. I think of all the fun and great people I've been able to meet over the years, just because I was chosen to be the voice of SpongeBob, because Stephen saw me as a kindred spirit with the character he'd created. Being the voice is a great calling card and conversation starter, and I'm always moved whenever someone turns to me and says, "You were the voice of my childhood."

CHAPTER 17

TOP FIVE EPISODE COUNTDOWN: NUMBER TWO

Our runner-up for the top slot—the number-two episode in our countdown of the top five—is a cartoon classic about cartooning.

An artist, portrayed by Mr. Lawrence (the voice of Plankton), sketching in a small boat at sea, loses his lone pencil overboard and triggers the iconic episode "Frankendoodle" (season 2, episode 14). The episode is an homage to artists, illustrators, and animators. You know, the people responsible for bringing the characters on *Sponge-Bob SquarePants* to life.

The pencil lands in Bikini Bottom, right between SpongeBob and Patrick, who are playing Rock, Paper, Scissors by blowing bubbles to represent their choices. The pencil stands straight up, with the point buried in the sand. That's when Stephen Hillenburg and the writers reference Stanley Kubrick's epic science fiction film *2001: A Space Odyssey* (1968). With the pencil replacing the film's mysterious black monolith that fell from the sky, SpongeBob and Patrick mimic the wild and frightened reactions of the prehistoric people from Kubrick's story.

Recognizing it as a giant pencil, SpongeBob is the first one brave enough to touch it and begins drawing. He sketches a crude jellyfish in the sand, with Patrick suddenly becoming savant Patrick. "It's lacking basic construction, and your perspective leaves a lot to be desired," says the erudite starfish, before his normally limited intelligence returns.

"Everyone's a critic," says SpongeBob, speaking for the artists on the show.

The jellyfish drawing comes to life, and the pair realize they've discovered a magic pencil. Eventually, SpongeBob, wanting to prank Squidward, sketches a copy of himself (one that resembles his forerunner, Sponge Boy). Its name is DoodleBob. Only DoodleBob, unlike our protagonist, appears to be an angry soul. He trashes Squidward and runs off with the magic pencil.

"Maybe he's in that poorly drawn pineapple," says Patrick, pointing to a sketched replica of SpongeBob's house. DoodleBob goes on a rampage with the pencil, causing complete havoc. Then SpongeBob regains control of it and erases all of DoodleBob, except for one arm.

That night, the arm sneaks into the pineapple and steals the pencil, redrawing himself. In a nod to the cult science fiction film *Invasion of the Body Snatchers* (1956), DoodleBob aims the pencil's eraser at our protagonist and proclaims, "You Doodle, me SpongeBob!"

With the pineapple and SpongeBob in jeopardy of being totally erased, DoodleBob accidentally steps onto a blank sheet of paper and sticks there. Seeing this, SpongeBob grabs a book off the shelf, opening it wide.

"Page for Mr. Doodle," he says, slamming DoodleBob shut inside.

When SpongeBob looks inside, DoodleBob's anger is gone. He's suddenly happy and at home on the page, as any drawing would be.

"He was just a two-dimensional creature lost in our three-dimensional aquatic world, longing for a purpose," SpongeBob explains to Patrick.

The pair send the magic pencil back to the surface. It lands in the boat from whence it came, where the excited artist now has a tool with which to draw. But in a beautifully constructed Rod Serling (*The Twilight Zone*) style ending, the artist breaks his pencil point.

That's right—he has no sharpener.

WHY IT GETS HIGH MARKS

In "Frankendoodle," Hillenburg creates a classic cartoon about cartooning. It's absurdly fun, riveting, and epic in its battles of pencil versus eraser, real life versus animation, and doodles versus the regular cast of animated aquatics. Naturally, DoodleBob finds the perfect home in a near-flawless episode, while the artist topside in the boat is shaded in comic irony.

BIKINI BOTTOM SOCIETY

THE TOP OF THE BOTTOM

The undersea society of Bikini Bottom, teeming with different types of aquatic life (and one resident land squirrel), is an incredible cultural stew, mostly living in peaceful harmony. Of course, there is a police force, SWAT team, and a jail, so the inhabitants do occasionally stray from socially acceptable animated behavior. Mrs. Puff, for example, has been arrested several times due to SpongeBob's bad driving. But we can forgive that.

As in any society, not everyone is exactly content. One way the inhabitants express their views and make waves, both politically and socially, is through graffiti. SpongeBob sees this whenever he takes the trash out to the dumpster behind the Krusty Krab.

"Dumpster writing—the voice of the people," says SpongeBob.

What do they have to say? *Up with Bubbles! Down with Air! Nematoads Are People Too!* (nematoads, correctly spelled *nematodes*, are sea worms), and *Starfish Rool* (I wonder who misspelled that?). Then there are those individuals who would rather profess something more personal: *Dogfish Loves Catfish* (perhaps a pair of sea-crossed lovers from different sides of the mid-ocean ridge).

There are also curse words on the lips of Bikini Bottomites. In fact, SpongeBob reads one on the dumpster and has no idea what it means in the episode "Sailor Mouth" (season 2, episode 18).

"That's one of those sentence enhancers," Patrick mistakenly tells him. "You use it when you want to talk fancy. You just sprinkle it over anything you say and you got yourself a spicy sentence sandwich."

So SpongeBob liberally uses the word with the lunch crowd at the Krusty Krab and all *H-E-double-hockey-sticks* breaks loose. The audience never actually gets to hear that word, which ranks number eleven on the list of the thirteen that no aquatic should ever utter. Squidward thinks there are just seven foul words—that's Stephen Hillenburg and the writers' tribute to comedian George Carlin's famed "Seven Dirty Words" routine.

Are there any acceptable, less salty expressions in Bikini Bottom? Sure. There's "Barnacles!" "Oh, tartar sauce!" and "Holy shrimp!"

The residents also express themselves via bumper stickers on their vehicles. So just be careful not to tailgate anyone with a sticker that reads, "I brake for sea urchins."

Going to the movies is a great way to blow off steam in Bikini Bottom, and the main theater is called the Reef. There's also the Bikini Bottom Zoo, the Fry Cook Museum, which features the first fork to find the ocean depths, and the Fish Hook Museum. And don't forget the Disney-inspired Glove World, with rides and glove-like hats and balloons. Stuck at home? You can play a board game such as Eels and Escalators (a take-off on Chutes and Ladders).

For those who find that type of entertainment too tame, there's always the weekly poker game hosted by Mr. Krabs and Plankton. High rollers, referred to as "whales" by casino operators, can try their luck in the Bass Vegas gambling houses. Shooting dice or craps is a common game. But they don't call rolling two ones "snake eyes." Instead, it's "fish eyes."

The local newspaper, *The Bikini Times*, can be filled with important headlines such as "School Dropout Rates Soar" and "Global Ocean Warming." But for aquatics who prefer tabloid journalism, there's always *The Bikini Bottom Inquirer* and *Fake Science Monthly*. Other reading materials include *TV Guide* (in case you need to check the channel or time for *The Rockfish Files*), *Snail Jokes*, *Lobster Home Journal*, *Jellyfish Weekly*, *Boring Science Digest*, and *Fancy Living Digest* (which trumpets the lifestyle of the 1 percent: aquatics who have a pool inside their pool). Then there's TV's Action News, hosted by Realistic Fish Head, a male Atlantic bluefin tuna (someone inform this fish he's in the Pacific) who moves only his mouth.

Be careful when traversing the outskirts of town, including the teens who park up on Make-out Reef. There are gigantic electrified jellyfish, sea rhinoceroses (make sure to wear your anti-sea-rhinoceros undergarments), enormous antlered moose snails, and sea bears, who, among other things, become enraged by both bad clarinet playing (just ask Squidward) and wearing a sombrero in a goofy manner. No, I'm not kidding—check out "The Camping Episode" (season 3, episode 17).

THE MALL

Perhaps the local Barg'N-Mart, shaped like a pirate's treasure chest, feels the economic pinch due to the popularity of Bikini Bottom's four-story mall, especially with aquatic teens also treating it as a hangout and a mainstay for weekend and summer employment. Oh, yes, the mall is shaped like a huge cruise ship. Perhaps it's one that actually sank, and Bottomite merchants simply moved in. That's the mind of Stephen Hillenburg for you.

What to do at the mall? You can visit the food court and Hot Dog on a String, where the tubelike alternative to patties and burgers is tied together with string and the employees wear buckets on their heads. Does

Plankton know about this? The establishment's motto: "Try it with X-tra string." There's the oceanic chain Bangles and Dangles for preteens and teens who crave layers of affordable jewelry and trinkets. The alternative, Scorched Earth, offers those with Goth or emo sensibilities fishbone necklaces, spiked sea urchins, and spiked collars and wristbands.

Other outlets in the mall include Clammy Jams, Hat Fancy, Jelly Jeans, Books 'R' Us, Lipp Lipp Gloss (selling lip gloss to fish), Pets, Shoes, Junky Junks, Wigs, and the Muzak Store, selling background music that is perfect for a mall shopping experience and an animated TV series. For shoppers on a tight budget, there's the 99 Cents Store, 49 Cents Store, and, remarkably, 0 Cents Store. You can also use the ATM for First Nautical Bank or charge your purchase using a credit card called MasterCarp. But be careful, credit card companies usually charge sharklike interest rates. There is also a teen gang that calls the mall its own—the Sharks. But the bloated mollies who've taken the job as mall cops will keep you safe. Maybe.

It's a big mall, so if you get lost, don't worry. There are maps everywhere stating: "You are here."

To Hillenburg and the writing staff's credit, there is one member of Bikini Bottom living at the mall in a cardboard box. So the social affliction of homelessness has not escaped this underwater society.

LAY OF THE UNDERSEA LAND

For those of you studying city planning or topography, here's a quick look at Bikini Bottom and its neighboring cities. You can view it all from the spectacular heights of the Sea Needle or via a flight arriving at or departing from the Bikini Bottom Airport.

Most picturesque towns have a Main Street running centrally, and Bikini Bottom is no different. Conch Street serves as its main street, being the home of SpongeBob, Patrick, and Squidward. It intersects with Barnacle Road and Coral Avenue. Anchor Way and Mr. Krabs's house aren't far off, and the Krusty Krab is appropriately situated on Bottomfeeder Lane.

Sections of town include Downtown Bikini Bottom, Goo Lagoon (where you might catch surfing legend Grubby Grouper hanging ten or however many digits he has), Sand Mountain, Jellyfish Fields, the Kelp Forrest, Residents Row, Make-out Reef, Ancient Mariner's Valley (Neptune's Paradise), Palm Bay, and the wealthy sections of Bottoms Up/ Waverly Hills above the Kelp Forrest cliffs.

On a note of finality, there's a crematorium in Bikini Bottom as well as a cemetery. Buried there are dearly departed Bottomites, along with Squidward's hopes and dreams of becoming a star, to which he regularly visits with flowers.

Of course, every now and then, the Bikini Bottom map has to be re-drawn to accommodate an unfolding adventure for SpongeBob and his friends—and, perhaps more importantly, the needs of the writers planning the next storyline. So don't become too miffed when things change places or shift slightly out of focus. In this animated world, imagination and not being bound by the past is the key to progress.

QUIZ QUESTION 18

What's the name of the Bikini Bottom cemetery? (The answer will bring back memories if you've ever experienced the death of a pet fish.)

The answer can be found after the book's conclusion.

CHARACTER ASSOCIATION

It's time to look deep within your psyche to determine whether you're a SpongeBob or a Squidward.

1. Would you rather make krabby patties over a hot grill or handle cold cash at the register?
2. Is blowing soap bubbles into different shapes or painting a self-portrait your idea of art?
3. Do you see a drinking glass as half full or the liquid inside as a choking hazard?
4. Would you rather sing to yourself while running through Jellyfish Fields or play the clarinet in a concert hall?

That might have been way too easy. Let's dig a little bit deeper and discover whether you're a Patrick or a Sandy.

1. Would you rather take an afternoon nap on a sun-warmed rock or go rock climbing on Mount Climb-up and Fall-off?
2. Is your idea of a five-star invention a glove to keep your hand clean of melting ice cream dripping down the side of a cone or a sustainable underwater peanut farm?
3. Would you rather break the Bikini Bottom record for consecutive belches or for hang gliding from the extreme height of the Sea Needle?
4. Do you consider it more fun to conjugate the word "wambo" or name a new type of undersea plant life?

It's time for you to decide whether you're a Plankton or a Mr. Krabs. So hold on tight to both your ego and your sense of self-worth.

1. Would you rather brainwash your customers or charge them extra for ice cubes in their soft drinks?
2. Is your goal to become big enough to ride the extreme roller coaster or to be the one selling tickets for the ride?
3. Would your perfect afternoon be spent sitting upon the throne of world domination or sinking the business of a rival competitor?
4. Are you better at creating semi-evil schemes or finding creative ways to frustrate them?

THE NUMBER-ONE EPISODE

PERSPECTIVE: TOM KENNY

Q: What's your favorite episode of *SpongeBob SquarePants*?

TK: It's next to impossible for me to choose my favorite episode. There are a lot of them that I love, and after so many years there are some great ones that I have forgotten. There are even some that I've only seen once or so, and it's like, "Oh yeah, this is great." But remember, the relationship of the cast to the episode can often be granular, because we're doing them one step at time, from storyboard, to voices and animation, to a finished product. So you can often lose sight of the episode as a whole, with it being such a collaborative effort between people and process.

TOP FIVE EPISODE COUNTDOWN: NUMBER ONE

Tom Kenny may not be able to choose his favorite episode, but I can. The number-one episode on my top-five countdown is . . . drumroll and nose-flute please . . . "The Idiot Box" (season 3, episode 4). It is the episode that has supplied us with the recurring section titled I-M-A-G-I-N-A-T-I-O-N that has appeared throughout many of these chapters.

When a Bikini Bottom mail truck delivers a huge box to an excited SpongeBob and Patrick, Squidward, who's watching from the front door of his Easter Island head abode, conjectures, "Probably ordered a lifetime supply of bubble soap." But there's no such sarcastic truth to that thought. Instead, there's a huge color TV inside. And Squidward does a double take when his annoying neighbors keep the empty box and put the TV into the trash. An instant later, an elated SpongeBob and Patrick jump inside the box and close the flaps.

"Let me get this straight," says Squidward, approaching the box. "You two ordered a giant-screen television just so you could play in the box?"

"Pretty smart, huh?" answers SpongeBob.

"I thought it wouldn't work," adds Patrick.

Squidward is incensed by what he believes is their abject stupidity.

But SpongeBob assures him that no one needs television as long as they have their imagination, a small rainbow suddenly stretching between SpongeBob's hands to illuminate the sentiment. The disbelieving Squidward sees this as the perfect opportunity to get himself a free giant TV and takes it back to his home.

Squidward goes inside to watch TV while SpongeBob and Patrick play mountain climbing adventure inside the closed cardboard container (yes, a cardboard box under water; just suspend your own disbelief). After coming outside to find the TV's remote, Squidward hears the most remarkable sounds coming from the box, as if his neighbors really were on a mountaintop.

"Patrick, I think we should keep our voices down. We might start an avalanche," SpongeBob warns his climbing companion. That's when Squidward kicks the box, resulting in the tumultuous sounds of an avalanche coming from inside.

A concerned Squidward hears his friends shrieking in pain, considering the idea of sawing off their limbs to free themselves from the ice and snow. Squidward hurriedly opens the box only to discover his friends sitting there contently.

"How are you two making those noises?" asks Squidward.

The answer is rather simple: a box and imagination. But he still has his doubts about that.

Squidward marches into his house and sits in a small hatbox to satisfy his own curiosity. Nothing happens. No fantasy. No adventure. Then he hears the sounds of police sirens outside and rushes into his yard. It's SpongeBob and Patrick, still in their box.

Next comes the sounds of a space launch. Squidward opens their box and demands to know, "Where's the tape recorder?" But there is none, just a small tape recorder box. Genius!

Climbing into the box with them, Squidward asks to be taken on an adventure to Robot Pirate Island, where he can arm wrestle with cowboys on the moon. His partners close their eyes and are both suddenly there. As for Squidward, though, he remains sitting in the now-empty box.

Later, pacing the floor of his home, a frustrated Squidward wonders, "How do those two work that thing?"

When SpongeBob and Patrick retire for the night, Squidward sneaks into the box alone. "Do I really believe that if I sit here and pretend to drive a race car that I'm suddenly going to start hearing noises?" As Squidward puts his tentacles on the imaginary wheel, those sounds magically begin.

"This beats TV by a long shot!" exclaims Squidward. "This is the most fun I've ever had!"

Ironically, it's not Squidward's imagination kicking in at all. A garbage truck has picked up the box with him still inside of it. That's the engine sound he hears. And that truck is heading toward the Bikini Bottom dump. Magnificent!

WHY IT GETS HIGH MARKS

This is one of a handful of the best animated cartoons I've ever seen. It's so simple yet completely enthralling. Stephen Hillenburg paints imagination as life's tour de force, a way of keeping reality in proper balance with a wide world of possibilities. With it, we can go anywhere and do anything, even from within the confines of an empty cardboard box. Both SpongeBob and Patrick possess that magic, but poor Squidward stumbles along, trying to find it. And just when Squidward thinks he's on the right track, he has to start over. "The Idiot Box" is sweet, funny, and complex in its simplicity.

CONCLUSION

My wife, April, and I watched hundreds of *SpongeBob SquarePants* episodes with our daughter, Sabrina. Sometimes I wondered exactly who was more entranced by the series, the adults or the child in our house. But whenever the backs of the adults were turned for a moment, we completely trusted that SpongeBob and his Bikini Bottom crew, including Stephen Hillenburg and Tom Kenny, were delivering something fun and oftentimes meaningful. And the one defining trait about SpongeBob that never seems to get old, no matter your age, is his desire for friendship. All that yellow sponge wanted was to be your friend. I think the rest of us wanted the same thing too.

QUIZ ANSWERS

1. SpongeBob informs Sandy that his middle name is "Air."
2. Patrick screams, "Merry Christmas!"
3. The theme song begins and ends with the sound of seagulls.
4. There are three palm trees on that model of an island.
5. Patrick wakes up to eat a krabby patty.
6. The word is "Loser."
7. Her twin brother is named Randy Cheeks.
8. Mr. Krabs stores barrels of root beer in his cellar. Pearl and her friends watch *Slumber Party Zombie Attack.*
9. SpongeBob's mom, Margaret SquarePants, doesn't wear glasses.
10. The license plate reads: IM-RDY. There is no zip code listed for Bikini Bottom.
11. Their burger stand was at the dump.
12. Not only is SpongeBob left-handed, but he states that he has *two* left hands.
13. SpongeBob has seven holes on his front facade, and both of his socks have a blue stripe over a red stripe.

14. Gary's shell is pink with purple dots and a red swirl. His two-toned shoes are brown and white.
15. "Mermaid Man and Barnacle Boy unite!"
16. SpongeBob counts the sesame seeds at 3:00 a.m.
17. Tiny Tim sings "Having a Wonderful Time."
18. Bikini Bottom's burial ground is Floater's Cemetery.

ACKNOWLEDGMENTS

Special thanks to Sabrina Volponi, April Volponi, Jim Nenopoulos, Tom Kenny, Christen Karniski, Samantha Delwarte, Lenny Shulman, and Joseph Miller.

NOTES

CHAPTER 1. HAPPY, YELLOW, AND SQUARE (EVENTUALLY)

1. All Tom Kenny quotes included in this book originate from an interview with Paul Volponi conducted on January 3, 2023.

CHAPTER 2. BECOMING SPONGEBOB

1. Stephen Hillenburg, *SpongeBob SquarePants* pitch bible, 1996, https://spongebob.fandom.com/wiki/SpongeBob_SquarePants_(pitch_bible)/gallery.

CHAPTER 3. THE THEME SONG

1. Joe D'Angelo, "Avril Lavigne Gives Squishy SpongeBob Song a Harder Edge," MTV.com, November 4, 2004 (accessed November 5, 2022).
2. Daniel Chavkin, "Why Guardians' Oscar Gonzalez Uses SpongeBob Theme as Walk-up Song," SI.com, October 7, 2022 (accessed October 8, 2022).

3. Bally Sports Ohio & Great Lakes, "Steven Kwan, Oscar Gonzalez, and Amed Rosario/Cleveland Guardians ALDS Game 3 Postgame Reaction," YouTube.com, October 16, 2022 (accessed October 16, 2022).

CHAPTER 7. SANDY CHEEKS

1. Laura Duphiney, interview by Paul Volponi, February 1, 2023.

INDEX

ABOUT THE AUTHOR

Sammy and SpongeBob.
Paul Volponi

Paul Volponi is a multi-award-winning author and journalist who has written twenty books, with an emphasis on books for young adults. He is the recipient of a dozen American Library Association honors. His previous books for Rowman & Littlefield include *Streetball Is Life: Lessons Learned on the Asphalt* and *Superhero Smart: Real-Life Facts behind Comic Book Characters.* Paul tours the country presenting at schools and conducting writing workshops. You can visit him at https://paulvolponibooks.com.